all about
knitting

all about knitting

Martingale®
Create with Confidence

![Martingale logo]

Martingale

Create with Confidence

Martingale®
19021 120th Ave. NE, Ste. 102
Bothell, WA 98011-9511 USA
ShopMartingale.com

First published as *How to Knit* in Great Britain in 2008 by Hamlyn, a division of Octopus Publishing Group Ltd 2–4 Heron Quays, London E14 4JP
www.octopusbooks.co.uk

Some of the material in this book has previously appeared in *The Knitter's Handbook* or in *Easy Knits,* both published by Hamlyn.

ISBN 978-1-60468-434-6

A CIP catalogue record for this book is available.

Printed and bound in China

18 17 16 15 14 13   8 7 6 5 4 3 2 1

Picture acknowledgements

Cover photography: © **Octopus Publishing Group Limited;** /Vanessa Davies front top left, front top center left, front top right, front bottom right, back right, spine; /Gareth Sambidge front bottom left, back left; /Joey Toller front top center right.

Commissioned photography © **Octopus Publishing Group**/Sandra Lane.

All other photography © **Octopus Publishing Group Limited**/Adrian Pope 72; /Andy Komorowski 1, 12, 18, 19, 24, 25, 27, 33, 40, 45, 57, 60, 61, 64, 66, 67, 77, 80, 82, 166, 170, 171,172, 173, 174, 175, 176, 177, 178, 179, 180, 181, 182, 183, 184, 185, 186,187, 188; /Janine Hosegood 14, 74, 75; /Joey Toller 98, 99, 116, 117, 119, 124, 132, 133, 162, 163, 164, 165; /Vanessa Davies 2, 4, 6, 8, 11, 12, 15, 22, 38, 48, 58, 68, 71, 78.

Credits

Executive Editor: Katy Denny
Senior Editor: Lisa John
Design Manager: Tokiko Morishima
Designer: Ben Cracknell Studios
Photographer: Sandra Lane
Illustrator: Kuo Kang Chen
Pattern Checker: Sue Horan
Picture Library Assistant: Ciaran O'Reilly
Senior Production Controller: Manjit Sihra

A note on buying yarn

When possible, the yarn brand recommended in the pattern should be used. If substituting yarn, it is recommended that you find one of a similar thickness and weight and that you knit a gauge swatch to check the stitch size and the drape of the fabric.

Yarn is dyed in batches and dye lots can vary greatly. It is essential to check the dye lot number on the yarn label of all balls of yarn used for the main color of the knitted project to make sure they are from the same dye lot.

Yarn manufacturers change the colors of the yarns they produce on a regular basis. If you are unable to find the exact colors suggested in the patterns in this book, your yarn supplier should be able to help you find a close match.

Mission Statement

Dedicated to providing quality products and service to inspire creativity.

Contents

Abbreviations

alt alternate

approx approximate(ly)

beg begin(ning)

bo bind off

cm centimeter(s)

co cast on

cont continu(e)(ing)

dec decreas(e)(ing)

DK double-knitting-weight yarn

EOR every other row

foll follow(s)(ing)

g gram(s)

in inch(es)

inc increas(e)(ing)

K knit

LH left hand

M1 make 1: pick up strand between stitch just worked and next stitch on LH needle and knit into back of it

mm millimeter(s)

oz ounce(s)

P purl

PU pick up and knit

patt pattern *or* work in pattern

psso pass slipped over stitch

rem remain(ing)

rep repeat

RH right hand

RS right side

sl slip

st(s) stitch(es)

St st stockinette stitch (knit on RS rows, purl on WS rows)

tbl through back of loop(s)

tog together

WS wrong side

wyib with yarn in back of work

wyif with yarn in front of work

yd yard(s)

yo yarn over

Introduction

Knitting has great appeal. There are numerous patterns and yarns to choose from and the techniques, once mastered, are easy. You don't need to set aside a huge amount of space to knit in, nor do you need any expensive or sophisticated equipment. This is a relaxing pastime, and one that you can easily pick up and put down wherever and whenever it suits you.

Newcomers to knitting will find this book the perfect resource. Split into two main sections – techniques and projects – the various chapters offer the beginner a comprehensive introduction to knitting from casting on the first stitch to producing clothes and accessories of the very highest quality. The information is presented clearly and logically, with the knitter's skill level increasing chapter by chapter.

You start at the very beginning with the most basic techniques of casting on, knitting and purling, and binding off. Once you have mastered these, it is simply a question of learning to follow a pattern before moving on to more advanced techniques such as knitting special textures (bobbles, cables, and loops), knitting in the round, working in more than one color, and adding embellishments (beads, tassels, and crocheted edges). You will also find instruction on adding zippers, hems, and pockets.

By the time you complete the techniques section you will be well versed in all of the steps needed to take on a whole project, and there are plenty of beautiful pieces to choose from in the chapters that follow. Here you will find winter-warming clothes for friends and family – from cute baby slippers and a child's rugged hoodie, to gorgeous pullovers, hats, gloves, and scarves. There are nursery favorites, including a blanket for a newborn baby and a soft knitted bunny and additional accessories including bags and cushions.

At the end of the book you will find a gallery of swatches, showing exactly how each stitch type looks when knitted – the perfect, instant reference when choosing a pattern of your own.

If you've never knitted before, the idea of transforming a ball of yarn into a beautifully knitted garment may seem daunting, but knitting is actually very easy. This section provides information on yarn types and the simple, inexpensive equipment you need for knitting. It shows you how to master the knit and purl stitches, and how to cast on and bind off. These most basic techniques will provide you with a solid foundation for all your future knitting projects.

The basics

Yarns

The yarn you use contributes to the pleasure of knitting as well as to the success of the finished piece. Knitting by hand is a very tactile activity, and a yarn that is both pleasing to touch and appropriate for the project will add to your enjoyment of the work and your pride in finishing a garment. There are many yarns to choose from – not only the classic smooth yarns, which never go out of fashion – but also a dazzling variety of unusual textures and fibers, from glossy silk, to velvety chenille, to chunky bouclé. The wide variety of yarns offers endless creative possibilities and is a good reason for learning to design your own patterns. Even if you use published patterns, as most beginners do, familiarity with the different yarns available will only enhance your experience, making you better able to choose the right yarn time and again.

Fiber content

Yarns are made from many different fibers and combinations of fibers, both natural and synthetic.

Natural fibers

Wool is the traditional favorite among natural fibers. It is warm and relatively lightweight. It also has an elastic quality, which makes it easy to knit and means that, if cared for properly, the finished garment holds its shape. Many wools are now machine washable.

Wool varies considerably in texture, depending on the breed of sheep it comes from and the spinning and finishing methods used. The softest quality is Merino wool, which comes from merino sheep. Lambswool is also very soft, since it comes from the first shearing of the young animals.

Mohair is the fluffy hair of the angora goat. Despite its delicate appearance, it is strong, though not very elastic. Kid mohair is softer than ordinary mohair from the adult animal and it tends to be more expensive. For economy, mohair is often combined with other fibers, such as wool or acrylic.

Angora is the fur of the angora rabbit and is feather-soft. Because it has a tendency to shed, it is not recommended for garments for babies, who might choke on the fibers.

Cashmere comes from the Himalayan or Cashmere goat. An extremely soft, luxurious, and warm fiber, it is sometimes blended with other fibers.

Alpaca is the hair of the alpaca. It is often added to wool yarns to provide extra softness.

Silk, which is spun from the cocoon of the silkworm, is a luxurious fiber with a strength that belies its softness.

Pure silk yarn normally has a glossy finish and comes in beautifully rich colors. Silk is also found combined with other fibers, including wool and mohair, to give the yarn more elasticity.

Cotton comes from the seed heads of the cotton plant. Cotton yarns are cool and are therefore ideal for summer garments.

Cotton that has been mercerized is particularly strong and lustrous. The only drawbacks with cotton yarn are its lack of elasticity, which makes it rather difficult to knit with, and its density, which makes it slow to dry after laundering.

Linen is a very strong fiber, taken from the stem of the flax plant. It has a naturally slubbed texture and is often combined with cotton.

Synthetic fibers

Synthetic fibers have many practical advantages over most natural ones; they are strong, lightweight, resistant to moths and, in many cases, machine washable. For these reasons, they are often added to natural fibers.

The main synthetic fibers are **acrylic**, **polyamide**, (including nylon), **polyester,** and **viscose** (including rayon). Of these, the most common is acrylic, which is very soft and lightweight. Acrylics are sometimes used to create novel textures that are not achievable with natural fibers. A special category of synthetic is the **metallic fibers**, which are derived from aluminium.

Yarns made of 100% synthetic fibers tend to be less satisfying to use than those made of natural fibers, or that are a natural-synthetic blend. They are less pleasing to the touch, and garments made from them are more likely to lose their shape.

This assortment of yarns gives an idea of the wide variety of textures available.

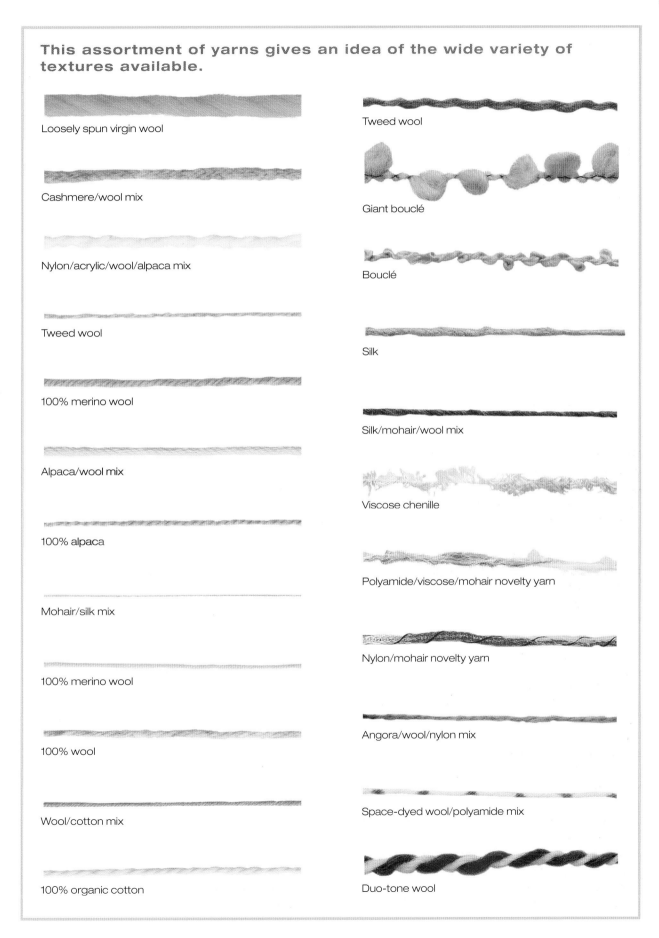

Loosely spun virgin wool

Cashmere/wool mix

Nylon/acrylic/wool/alpaca mix

Tweed wool

100% merino wool

Alpaca/wool mix

100% alpaca

Mohair/silk mix

100% merino wool

100% wool

Wool/cotton mix

100% organic cotton

Tweed wool

Giant bouclé

Bouclé

Silk

Silk/mohair/wool mix

Viscose chenille

Polyamide/viscose/mohair novelty yarn

Nylon/mohair novelty yarn

Angora/wool/nylon mix

Space-dyed wool/polyamide mix

Duo-tone wool

Yarn construction

The character of a yarn is determined not only by its fiber content, but also by the spinning and finishing methods used in its manufacture.

Size

Yarns vary enormously in size, or thickness (also called their "weight"). The smooth, so-called "classic" yarns can be broken down into seven general weights: lace-weight, fingering weight, sport-weight double knitting, Aran-weight, chunky and bulky. There is some variation within these categories, but it is usually possible to substitute one yarn for another as long as it is in the same category.

The word "ply" is used in two ways. Literally, it means an individual strand of fiber. A ply can be of any thickness; therefore, a yarn consisting of two plies could be thicker than one containing four. Textured yarn may also be described in relation to these categories; for example, "knits as DK-weight" means that the yarn (irrespective of its construction) will yield roughly the same number of stitches and rows over a given measurement as a standard DK-weight yarn. This information is useful if you are substituting a yarn or designing a garment from scratch.

Some basic weights of smooth yarn

Sport (100% alpaca)

Double knitting (DK) (100% cotton)

Aran (55% merino, 33% microfibre, 12% cashmere)

Chunky (100% alpaca)

Bulky (50% wool, 50% alpaca)

Finish

Fibers undergo a number of different finishes during the spinning process. They may be twisted loosely or firmly, for example, to produce a wide range of textures, from soft to very firm. In general, the tighter the twist, the harder-wearing the yarn.
Slubbed yarns are spun irregularly, so that they have thick and thin stretches. They add a pleasing variation of texture to plain stitch patterns, but are less successful than smooth yarns when worked in complex stitch patterns because they tend to obscure the finer detail. Slubbed yarns can be quite effective in some larger lace and cable patterns, however.
Bouclé yarns have a crinkly texture, which is produced by catching up one of the plies so that it forms a little loop around the other(s).

Yarns are available in a variety of weights, plies, and finishes.

Understanding yarn label symbols

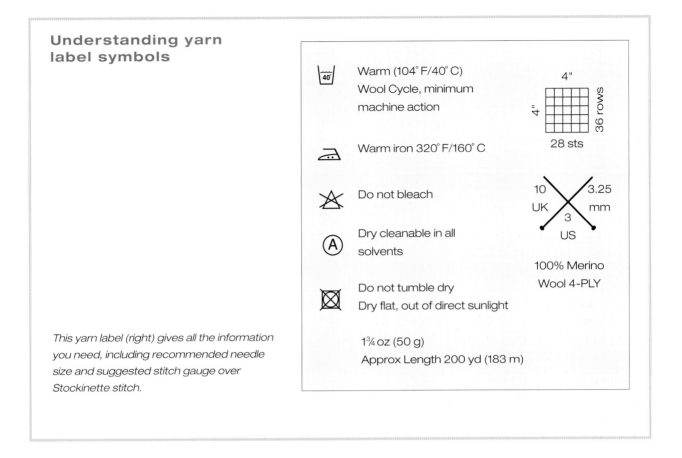

Warm (104° F/40° C) Wool Cycle, minimum machine action

Warm iron 320° F/160° C

Do not bleach

Dry cleanable in all solvents

Do not tumble dry Dry flat, out of direct sunlight

4"
4"
36 rows
28 sts

10 UK   3.25 mm
3
US

100% Merino Wool 4-PLY

1¾ oz (50 g)
Approx Length 200 yd (183 m)

This yarn label (right) gives all the information you need, including recommended needle size and suggested stitch gauge over Stockinette stitch.

Knop yarns are similar in construction to bouclé yarns, but are more irregular, with large loops at more widely spaced intervals. They produce a fuzzy, knobbly fabric. **Chenille yarns** have a dense, velvety texture. Although very attractive, they are not easy to knit with because they tend to stretch out of shape, or "worm." **Multicolored effects** can be produced by spinning together plies of different colors, or, for a subtler effect, different shades of the same color. Flecked tweed yarns are the classic example of a multicolored yarn. Space-dyed yarn where the color changes along its length, is fun to use, although the results can be unpredictable. **Novelty yarns** appear and disappear along with the latest trends. They may include woven ribbon and rag yarns, blends of metallic and cotton fibers, thin strands of suede – whatever is currently in vogue.

The choice of yarns available is dictated to some extent by fashion and it used to be the case that, when color-patterned knitting became voguish, the more unusual textures, which do not lend themselves to such designs, were less commonly available. The internet has done much to remedy this, however, and it is now possible to source yarns of all types throughout the year and regardless of the latest trends.

Buying yarn

When buying yarn, it is very important to read the information on the yarn label. This information will include the fiber content, blocking/pressing instructions, recommendations on how to care for the garment, and the weight of the ball or skein. In some cases it may also give a recommended needle size and the number of stitches and rows produced in stockinette stitch using those needles (see Gauge, page 25). This last information is very useful if you wish to substitute a different yarn for the one recommended by the pattern you are using.

One essential piece of information on the yarn label is the dye-lot number. Make sure that all the yarn for any one garment is from the same lot – even a minor variation can be quite noticeable. Buy all the yarn you need at the same time, because the particular dye lot you are using may no longer be available later on if you should run out.

Equipment

You do not need a vast array of special equipment for hand knitting. The only essential items, of course, are the needles. Needles come in a variety of sizes (see page 189) and types, and you can build up a useful collection as you build on your skills. There are also a number of accessories that will come in handy occasionally.

Needles are made of several different materials: metal, plastic, bamboo, and wood are all commonly available. Metal needles are generally the easiest to work with, as the stitches slide along them easily; plastic tends to be rather sticky, although some people prefer them because they are warmer to the touch. Circular needles have rigid points that are attached to a flexible length of cord. These are useful for knitting heavy items, as it means you do not have to support the whole weight of the garment yourself as you work, as well as, for working in the round.

Other types of needle include double-pointed needles, for working in the round, and cable needles, used in cable-stitch patterns.

If you take good care of your needles they should last for many years. Store them in a large flat box or special needle case, so that they do not become bent. Never use a needle with a jagged point, as it can catch in the yarn, splitting the fibers.

Set of four double-pointed needles – used for tubular knitting (such as for socks and mittens) and for medallions

Cable needle – the bend prevents the held stitches from slipping off

Circular needle – used for knitting in the round or straight knitting

Tape measure – used for checking that your worked pieces are of the correct gauge.

Ring stitch markers – used to mark the beginning of rounds in circular knitting and certain key points in a stitch pattern

Stitch stoppers or needle guards – used to prevent the work from slipping off the needle when it is put away; an elastic band will serve the same purpose, but stoppers will also protect the needle points

Knitter's pins – used for holding two knitted sections together when seaming and for marking divisions on edges when picking up a specified number of stitches

Glass-headed pins – used for blocking knitting

Blunt-ended yarn needle – used for seams and for working embroidery on knitting

Bobbin – used for holding small amounts of yarn when working with two or more colors across a row

Stitch holder – a double-pointed needle or a length of yarn will also work; knitter's safety pins are best where only a few stitches need to be held

Needle gauge – useful for checking sizes of double-pointed and circular needles (marked only on the package) and when using needles sized according to a different system from the one used in the pattern

Other useful equipment includes a row counter for keeping track of the number of rows worked, scissors, a spray bottle for wet blocking, an iron, a cotton pressing cloth and an ironing board with a well-padded surface. A knitting bag is handy for keeping your knitting clean and tidy; some bags have wooden frames that allow them to stand on the floor when in use and fold up for carrying or storing. A folder for storing patterns is also useful.

Double-pointed needles are used to knit socks in the round.

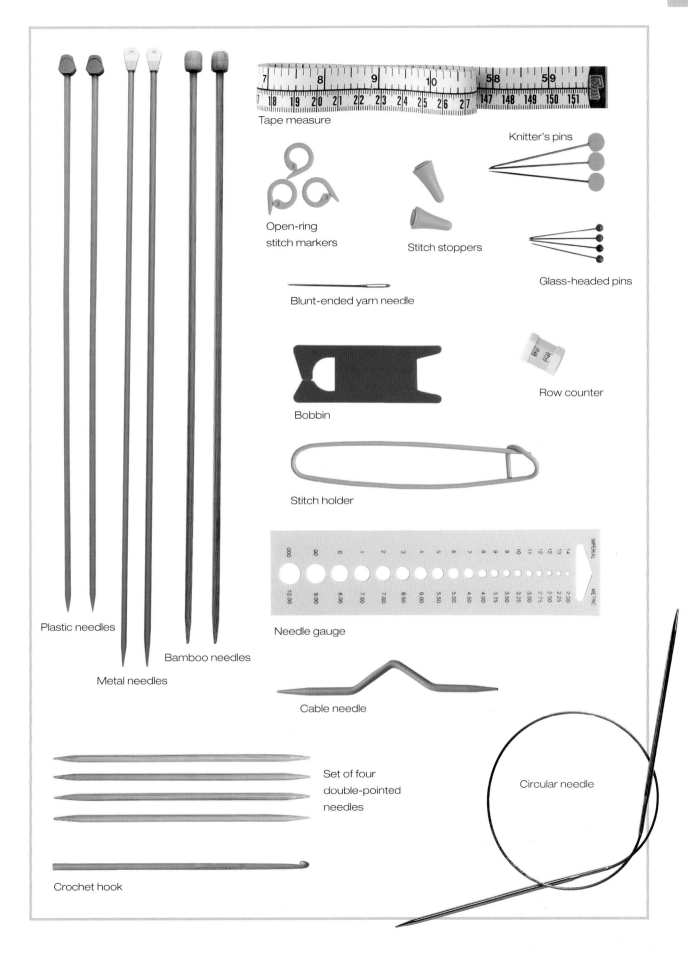

Tape measure

Open-ring
stitch markers

Stitch stoppers

Knitter's pins

Glass-headed pins

Blunt-ended yarn needle

Bobbin

Row counter

Stitch holder

Needle gauge

Plastic needles

Metal needles

Bamboo needles

Cable needle

Set of four
double-pointed
needles

Circular needle

Crochet hook

Casting on

The first step when starting a piece of knitting is to place the required number of stitches on the needle. This is called casting on. There are several different methods of casting on, the most common of which are the cable method and the thumb method. For both of these you need to hold the yarn as for knitting, so turn to page 18 to see which way of holding the yarn you prefer. The single cast-on is the simplest method; however, because the loops formed are difficult to work into evenly, it is not recommended for the novice. The double cast-on may look very complicated, but it has the benefit of needing no knitting experience. If you tend to cast on tightly, use needles a size or two larger than specified by the pattern for the casting on. Then change to the correct needles for the first row.

Slip knot

For the single cable and thumb cast-ons, begin by making a slip knot on the needle. First make a loop in the yarn and draw one end of the yarn through with the point of the needle. Pull on both ends of the yarn to tighten the knot.

Single cast-on

This method produces a soft, flexible edge. Begin by making a slip knot near the end of the yarn. Wind the yarn around the thumb, and hold it with three fingers.

1 Bring the needle up through the loop as shown by the arrow.

2 Slip the thumb out of the loop, and use it to pull the yarn gently downward, forming a stitch. Repeat steps 1 and 2.

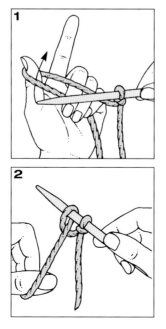

Cable cast-on

This method produces an attractive, smooth edge, which is suitable for various fabrics. Begin with a slip knot near the end of the yarn.

1 Holding the loose end of the yarn firmly, insert the right-hand (RH) needle under the left-hand (LH) needle, to the left of the slip knot. Take the main yarn under and over the RH needle, from left to right.

2 Draw the loop on the RH needle through to the front, and place it over the top of the LH needle.

3 Insert the RH needle between the two stitches. Take the yarn under and over the needle, as in step 2, draw the loop through, and place it on the needle. Repeat step 3.

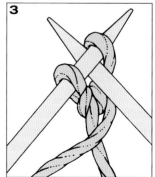

Thumb cast-on

The edge produced by this method is the same as for the double cast-on. Multiply the number of stitches by ¾" (2 cm) and measure off this length of yarn; make a slip knot slightly beyond this point. Hold the short end of yarn in your left hand as shown. Wrap the yarn from the ball around the little finger of your right hand, as for knitting (see page 18).

1 Insert the point of the needle up under the front strand of yarn lying between the fingers and thumb of the left hand, following the direction of the arrow.

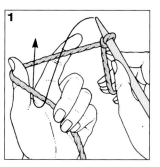

2 Bring the right-hand (ball) yarn under and over the point of the needle. Holding both lengths of yarn fairly taut, bring the needle down through the left-hand loop as shown by the arrow.

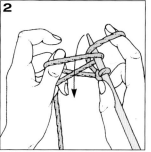

3 Slip the thumb out of the loop, and use it to pull on the short end of yarn as shown to complete the new stitch. Repeat steps 1–3.

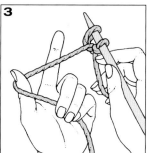

Double cast-on

Multiply the number of stitches required by ¾" (2 cm), and measure off this length of yarn. Wind the yarn around the fingers of your left hand as shown: up between the third and little fingers, around the little finger, over all four fingers, then clockwise around the thumb; finally take the yarn between the second and third fingers and hold it gently but firmly. Spread the thumb and index finger apart to apply tension to the yarn.

1 Slip the point of the needle up through the thumb loop.

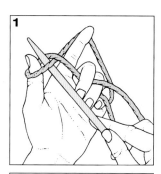

2 Take the needle over and under the yarn extending to the index finger, thus forming a loop on the needle; as you do so, rotate your left hand toward you. (You may do this instinctively, as it feels natural).

3 Bring the needle back through the thumb loop. Slip the thumb out of the loop and use it to pull down the free length of yarn. This completes the first stitch. Repeat steps 1–3. This produces a quite firm, yet flexible edge, which is good for ribbing.

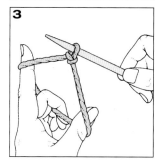

Holding the yarn

Once you have cast some stitches onto a needle, you are ready to begin knitting. There are several ways of holding the yarn and needles, and the two basic methods are shown here. The right-hand method of holding the yarn is used mainly in English-speaking countries, while the left-hand method is more commonly used in continental Europe. Each method produces the same results. Try both to see which you find more comfortable. It is a good idea to learn both methods, as for some multicolored knitting patterns you need to work with two different yarns at the same time. Whichever method you choose, wind the yarn loosely around the fingers to keep it slightly tensioned so that the stitches stay smooth and even. When starting out this may mean wrapping the yarn twice around your little finger.

Right-hand method

Hold the needle with the cast-on stitches in the left hand. Wind the yarn around the fingers of the right hand as shown below.

Hold the needle in the right hand so that it lies between the thumb and the rest of the hand as shown (in practice, the needle is often picked up before the yarn). Insert the needle into the first stitch on the LH needle, and slide the right hand forward to wrap the yarn around the point of the RH needle. In the photograph the needles are shown forming the knit stitch.

Left-hand method

Hold the needle with the cast-on stitches in the right hand. Wind the yarn around the fingers of the left hand as shown.

Transfer the needle with the stitches to the left hand, and raise the index finger to tension the yarn. Hold the working needle in the right hand, with the thumb in front and the fingers in back. Insert the needle into the first stitch, then rotate the left hand to bring the yarn around the point of the needle. In the photograph the needles are shown forming the knit stitch.

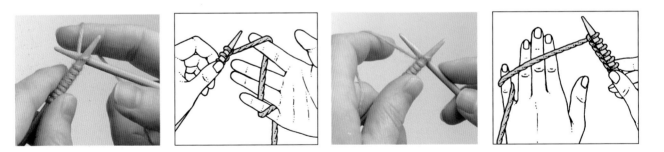

TIP

The right-hand method is often referred to as "English knitting," as it was more common in the UK. This method is also referred to as "throwing," because the knitter wraps, or throws, the working yarn around the needle to make a new stitch. The term "continental" is commonly used to describe the left-hand method as it is often associated with continental European knitters. This style of knitting is also called "picking," because rather than wrapping the yarn around the needle to make a stitch, the knitter uses the tip of the needle to pick up the working yarn and pull it through the stitch on the needle.

Knit and purl

Most knitting is based on combinations of just two basic stitches: the knit stitch and the purl stitch. Once you have mastered these two stitches, you can work many different stitch patterns. Begin by casting on 25 to 30 stitches, using a DK-weight yarn in a light color, preferably all wool or a wool blend for its resilience. Practice the knit stitch until you can work it smoothly. Then practice the purl stitch.

The knit stitch

1 Hold the needle with the stitches to be knitted in the left hand with the working yarn behind the work.

2 Insert the RH needle into a stitch from front to back. Wrap the yarn over the RH needle, forming a loop.

3 Bring the needle and the new loop to the front of the work, and slide the original stitch off the LH needle.

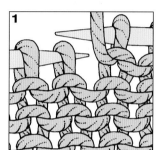

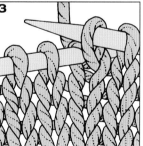

The purl stitch

1 Hold the needle with the stitches to be purled in the left hand, with the working yarn at the front of the work.

2 Insert the RH needle through the front of the stitch, from back to front. Wrap the yarn over and around the RH needle, forming a loop.

3 Pull the needle and the new loop through to the back; and slide the original stitch off the LH needle.

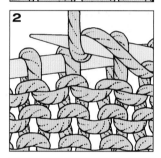

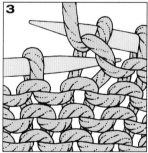

Garter stitch (right). This simple stitch pattern is produced by knitting every row. The fabric has a distinct horizontal ridge and is quite stretchy.

Stockinette stitch (right) is produced by knitting all the stitches on the right-side rows and purling on the wrong-side rows. The fabric is smooth and slightly elastic.

Stitch variations

Once you have mastered the knit and purl stitches, it is easy to learn a few variations on these basic techniques. One of these is working into the back of the stitch rather than into the front of it. You may use this technique when increasing stitches (see pages 28–30) and in some stitch patterns. It is possible to produce a variation of stockinette stitch by working all the knit stitches through the back; you work the purl stitches through the front as usual. The resulting fabric is unusually firm. Another technique is simply to slip a stitch off the left-hand needle on to the right without working it. Slipped stitches are used in some methods of decreasing (see page 32) and in some multicolor patterns (see page 61).

Knitting through the back of the loop (abbreviated K1 tbl)

Insert the RH needle behind the LH needle and through the back of the stitch, and wrap the yarn up and over the needle, forming a knit stitch in the usual way. Pull the new stitch through, and slip the original stitch off the LH needle. The new stitch is slightly twisted.

Slipping a stitch knitwise (abbreviated Sl 1 kw)

Insert the needle into the front of the stitch as if to knit it, but do not form a new stitch; simply slip the original stitch on to the RH needle. The same technique is used to slip a purl stitch knitwise. Unless the pattern instructions state otherwise, the yarn is held as for the preceding stitch: at the back for a knit stitch; at the front for a purl stitch.

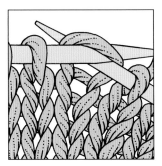

Purling through the back of the loop (abbreviated P1 tbl)

Turn the RH needle briefly to point from left to right, then insert it from back to front through the back of the loop as shown. Form a purl stitch in the usual way, and slip the original stitch off the LH needle. The new stitch is slightly twisted.

Slipping a stitch purlwise (abbreviated Sl 1 pw)

Insert the needle into the stitch from back to front, as if you were going to purl it, then simply slip it on to the RH needle. The same technique is used to slip a purl stitch purlwise. Unless the pattern states otherwise, the yarn is held as for the preceding stitch.

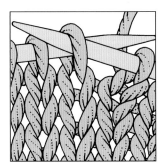

Binding off

To end a piece of knitting, you bind off the stitches. This technique is also used to reduce the number of stitches at the side of a piece of knitting – for example, when shaping an armhole – or in the middle when shaping a neckline or working a horizontal buttonhole. There are several methods of binding off, but the one shown here is most common. This basic method alters slightly when binding off a ribbed fabric, where it produces a softer, more elastic edge than the basic method. To avoid binding off too tightly, and producing an edge that is narrower than the width of the fabric, use a needle one or two sizes larger than those used for the main fabric. When you have learned the basic bind-off method, try the advanced methods on pages 82–83.

Basic bind-off
(abbreviated BO)

1 Knit the first two stitches. *Slip the LH needle into the first stitch on the RH needle.

2 Lift the first stitch over the second stitch and off the needle. Knit one more stitch and then repeat from * until one stitch remains. Break the yarn and draw it firmly through the last stitch.

If binding off on the purl side (the wrong side) of a stockinette stitch fabric, you may prefer to purl the stitches instead of knitting them. Here, the loops of the bound-off edge will lie toward the knit side of the work.

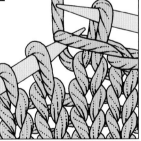

Binding off in rib

Work all the stitches as if continuing in the pattern: so purl stitches will be purled, rather than knitted. Lift the first stitch over the second as usual.

Achieving an even bind-off in rib is not easy, even for experienced knitters. Practice on a spare piece of ribbing, keeping a fairly loose tension and working evenly.

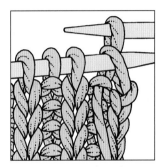

You might feel that you can knit and purl, but are not confident enough to follow a knitting pattern. It is true that patterns often look very complex and may even appear to be written in a foreign language. However, it is relatively easy to learn this language, as you are about to discover. All but the simplest projects contain increases, decreases, and seams, and many also require you to pick up stitches or make a buttonhole. All of these techniques are described on the following pages. And, most important for a beginner, there are instructions on correcting any mistakes you happen to make.

Following a pattern

Selecting a pattern

It's important to select a pattern that is appropriate for your level of ability so that it will be successful and encourage you to develop your knitting skills. If you are choosing your first pattern, try to select something that is not absolutely dependent on perfect sizing and shaping, such as a scarf or throw, or even a purse. Also, do not choose a very complicated stitch pattern.

Size

Check that the sizes given with a pattern include one that is suitable for your measurements. The bust measurement should allow some room for movement when wearing the garment, known as "ease." If several sets of measurements are given, the smallest size is always indicated first, with larger ones in parentheses. It is a good idea to circle each figure that refers to your size.

Materials and equipment

A printed pattern will specify all the materials and equipment necessary to complete the garment. It will state the amount and type of yarn and the needle sizes needed, the correct gauge (see page 25), and any extras required, such as buttons or zippers. While still learning to knit, it is wise to choose the exact yarn specified in the pattern. Later, when you are more experienced, you can often substitute a different yarn for the one specified. For guidance on selecting yarn, see pages 10–13.

Sequence of working

The pattern will indicate the order in which you should work the pieces. Always stick to this order. Often some instructions in one piece relate to those already completed. You should also sew the pieces together in the order suggested, because this may affect some further work such as adding a neckband or collar.

Get into the habit of checking your work as you go along, especially if it has a complicated stitch pattern. Lay it out flat in good light and look at it carefully. By checking the number of stitches on the needle you can quickly tell whether or not everything is going according to plan.

Knitting language

All knitting patterns use abbreviations and symbols of various kinds in order to save space. These are fairly standard, although you will find some differences in patterns and knitting books produced in different English-speaking countries. A full list of the abbreviations used in this book is given on page 6. Special abbreviations are explained at the beginning of a pattern.

In addition to abbreviations, patterns use symbols such as ( ), [ ], and * *. These may contain variations for different garment sizes, or they may enclose a set of instructions that are to be repeated. For example: *K1, P1, rep from * to end.

Sections of a pattern that are to be repeated may use two or more asterisks, to indicate repeats within repeats. Although this all sounds very confusing to the beginner, you will find as you gain experience that such symbols are very easy to understand.

Knitting a simple shape, such as a blanket, can provide a good opportunity to experiment with color and texture.

Gauge

A very important part of any knitting pattern is where it states the necessary gauge. The gauge refers to the number of stitches and rows, over a given measurement, obtained by the designer of that pattern. It will be given in a form such as: "21 sts and 30 rows to 4 inches (10 cm), measured over St st on 4 mm needles." Sometimes the gauge is measured "over pattern" – that is, over the stitch pattern used for the main part of the garment. It is essential to check your gauge in order for the garment to come out the correct size. The best way to do this, is to knit a swatch before beginning the garment itself.

Knitting a swatch

The gauge equals the number of stitches per inch, so cast on a few more stitches than are required to achieve 4" (10 cm), as listed in the project gauge. For example, if the gauge is given as "22 stitches = 4" (10 cm)," cast on 25 to 30 stitches. Work in stockinette stitch, unless another stitch pattern is specified, until swatch measures 4" (10 cm). Bind off the stitches.

Pin the swatch to a flat, padded surface, without stretching it. For highly textured or lacy patterns, it may be necessary to block the work (see page 35) to make it as smooth as the finished garment will be.

Measure the width of the knitted swatch and then divide the number of stitches you've cast on by the width of your swatch. For example, if your swatch measures 4½" (11.5 cm) and you've cast on 25 stitches, your swatch gauge is 5½ stitches per inch (25 sts ÷ 4.5 = 5.5). If the stitches per inch (gauge) is greater than your pattern calls for, switch to a larger size needle and knit a new swatch. If the gauge is smaller than your pattern calls for, try a smaller pair of needles.

It is a good idea to recheck your gauge during the course of knitting a garment, which you can do on a completed section.

Swatching complex stitch patterns

To make a swatch for a complex stitch pattern, look at the first row that contains a repeated group of stitches and calculate how many stitches are in the repeat. For example: *(K1, P1, K1) into first st, P3tog, rep from * to end. When you have followed the first instruction, in brackets, you will have 3 stitches; from the second, "purl 3 together," you will have 1 stitch. Add the 1 to the 3 to get the number of stitches in one repeat: 4.

The number of stitches to cast on must be divisible by 4 and include a few stitches more than those specified for the gauge. Add any edge stitches given in the pattern; these will be found outside the asterisks. Cast on this number and work as instructed until the swatch measures just over 4"(10 cm).

If the stitches are hard to count, tie loops of yarn at the beginning and end of the specified number of stitches and rows. Then measure the gauge between these markers.

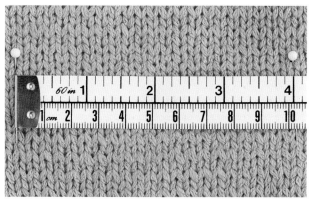

Measuring the distance between a given number of stitches on a knitted swatch will indicate if your gauge is too loose or too tight.

Correcting mistakes

It is a good idea to learn how to deal effectively with mistakes. Keep a crochet hook within easy reach, as you can use it to pick up dropped stitches. A cable needle or safety pin is also useful for holding a loose stitch while you deal with a problem. After correcting a mistake, always count the stitches to make sure you have the right number.

Picking up a dropped knit stitch

If the work is in stockinette stitch, insert the crochet hook from front to back through the lowest stitch in the ladder, pick up the strand as shown, and pull it through the loop on the hook to make a new stitch; repeat to the top of the ladder, and place the last stitch on the LH needle, making sure it is turned the same way as all other stitches and not twisted.

Unpicking stitches

If you find a mistake a few rows down, it is feasible to unpick the work stitch by stitch until you reach the mistake, then correct it and proceed as usual.

1 To unpick a knit stitch, put the LH needle through the stitch below. Pull the RH needle out of the stitch above it, and pull the yarn out of the loop.

2 To unpick a purl stitch, the process is essentially the same as for a knit stitch, but you hold the yarn in front of the work.

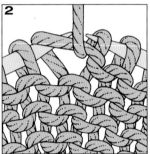

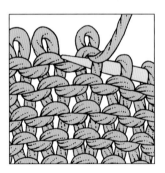

Picking up a dropped purl stitch

In some patterns you will need to pick up purl stitches when retrieving a ladder. The technique is basically the same as for a knit stitch, but you insert the hook from back to front as shown.

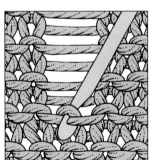

Unravelling

For a mistake more than a few rows down, unravel the work to one or two rows below the mistake, ending with the yarn at the RH edge. In some patterns it is easier to work from the right side of the fabric; in others, including stockinette stitch, it is easier to work on the wrong side, as shown.

Insert the needle into the stitch below the RH loop from back to front, and pull out the loop. Continue in this way to the end of the row.

When picking up stitches after unravelling, use a needle two or three sizes smaller than those used for the knitting to avoid pulling the stitches out of shape.

Selvages

A selvage is a specially worked edge on a piece of knitting. You may add one to give a smooth, firm edge on a fabric such as stockinette stitch, which would otherwise have a rather loose one, to make the edges easier to handle when sewing seams. Or you might use a selvage to give a decorative finish to a piece of knitting that is not going to have a seam – a scarf, for example. A selvage will also prevent the edges from curling.

Single chain edge

This selvage gives a smooth edge and is appropriate for pieces that will be joined edge to edge (see page 36) or where stitches will be picked up (see page 33).

For the right side: always slip the first stitch knitwise, work in pattern, and then knit the last stitch.

For the wrong side: always slip the first stitch purlwise, work in pattern, and then purl the last stitch.

Single garter edge

This method produces a firm edge on fabrics that tend to be loose, and is especially well suited to projects where you'll use backstitch seams (see page 36).

For both right and wrong sides: always knit the first and the last stitch on each row.

Double garter edge

This is a decorative edge that lies flat. It is worked on 2 stitches for each edge.

For both right and wrong sides: slip the first stitch knitwise and knit the second stitch. At the end of each row, knit the last 2 stitches.

Increases and decreases

There are many different methods of increasing and decreasing, and they are used for various purposes. You might use a series of increases or decreases at the edge of a piece of knitting or across a row to shape it. You might also use them decoratively to produce many interesting stitch patterns. When used for stitch patterns, increases and decreases are normally paired, so that the number of stitches on the needle remains the same.

Increasing

The three increases shown here and opposite are discreet and inconspicuous. The increases on page 30 are decorative increases, which make a hole in the fabric and are used mainly in lace patterns. They are produced by wrapping the yarn over or around the needle, depending on the starting position of the yarn.

Bar increase – knitwise

(abbreviated inc 1 or K1f&b)

A bar increase involves working twice into the same stitch. Whether worked on a knit row or a purl row, this produces a tiny horizontal strand, or bar, on the knit side of the work. If worked a few stitches in from the edge, it can have a decorative effect.

1 Knit into the front of the stitch as usual, but do not slip the stitch off the needle at this point. Instead, knit again into the same stitch through the back of the loop.

2 Slip the original stitch off the LH needle. Two stitches have been made from one. This method of increasing is often used to create fullness above the ribbing at the bottom of a sweater.

Bar increase – purlwise

(abbreviated inc 1 or P1f&b)

1 Purl the stitch in the usual way, but do not slip the stitch off the needle.

2 Purl again into the same stitch through the back of the loop – twisting the stitch as shown.

3 Slip the original stitch off the LH needle.

In either a knit or purl bar increase the little bar produced on the knit side will appear to the right of the first of the two stitches. Therefore, if you inc 1 into the 4th stitch from the RH edge, you should work across the row until there are 5 stitches remaining, and work the inc 1 into the first of these 5 stitches. On the knit side the bar will appear 4 stitches in from each edge.

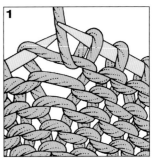
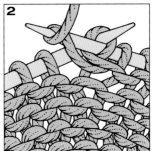

Making one knitwise stitch
(abbreviated M1)

1 Insert the LH needle from front to back under the strand lying between the two adjacent stitches on the LH and RH needles.

2 Knit into the back of the new loop just formed on the LH needle.

3 Slip the loop off the LH needle onto the RH needle.

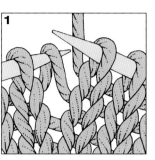

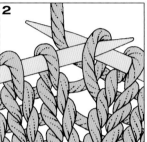

Making one purlwise stitch
(abbreviated M1)

1 Insert the LH needle from front to back under the strand lying between the two adjacent stitches on the LH and RH needles.

2 Purl into the back of the new loop just formed, twisting it as shown to make this possible.

3 Slip the picked-up loop off the LH needle onto the RH needle.

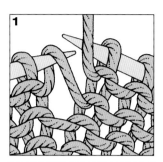

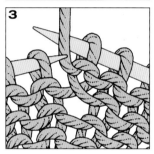

Lifted increase – knitwise

Like the M1 increase, this type of increase is inconspicuous.

1 With the RH needle, pull up the stitch lying directly below the next stitch on the LH needle, from front to back, and knit into it.

2 Knit into the next stitch on the LH needle.

Lifted increase – purlwise

1 With the RH needle, pull up the stitch lying directly below the next stitch on the LH, from back to front, and purl into it.

2 Purl into the next stitch on the LH needle.

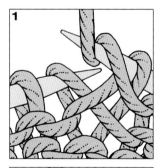

Yarn over

(abbreviated YO)

This is worked between two knit stitches.

1 Wrap the yarn from the front of the work, up and over the RH needle.

2 Knit the next stitch in the usual way – this will form an extra loop on the needle.

3 On the next row, purl into the yarn over loop as if it were a stitch (or work as instructed in the pattern).

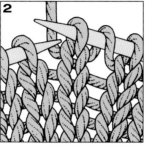

Yarn over variation

(abbreviated YO)

This yarn over is worked between a purl stitch and a knit stitch; the yarn will be at the front of the work. Wrap the yarn up and over the RH needle. Knit the next stitch in the usual way. On the next row, work into the new loop as instructed by the pattern.

Yarn over variation

(abbreviated YO)

This yarn over is worked between two purl stitches, or between a knit and a purl stitch. Begin with the yarn at the front of the work.

1 Wrap the yarn over the RH needle, and then bring it completely around the needle to the front of the work.

2 Purl the next stitch as usual – this will form an extra loop on the needle.

3 On the next row work into the loop as if it were a stitch.

The yarn over increase is used in creating eyelets, as in this quatrefoil eyelet pattern (see page 173).

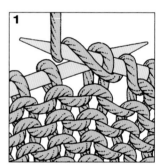

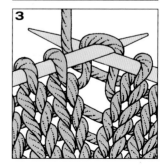

Decreasing

There are fewer methods of decreasing than of increasing. Like increases, however, each method produces a different effect on a fabric and can be used either inconspicuously to help shape the overall piece, or decoratively.

On raglan armholes a decorative type of decreasing called full-fashioned shaping is popular. Here, you work the decreases two stitches in from the edge. At the right-hand edge you work a slip-stitch decrease on the third and fourth stitches from the edge; at the left-hand edge you knit the third and fourth stitches together.

Knitting two stitches together
(abbreviated K2tog)

1 This is a right-slanting decrease. Insert the RH needle knitwise into the second stitch on the LH needle and then into the first stitch.

2 Knit the 2 stitches together, and then slip the original 2 stitches off the LH needle.

Purling two stitches together
(abbreviated P2tog)

1 This is a right-slanting decrease. Insert the RH needle purlwise into the first stitch on the LH needle and then into the second stitch.

2 Purl the 2 stitches together, and then slip the original 2 stitches off the LH needle.

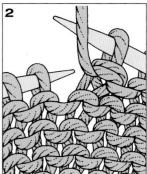

Knitting together through back loops
(abbreviated K2tog tbl)

This is a left-slanting decrease. When 2 stitches are knitted together normally, they slant to the right. For patterns that require a slant to the left, insert the RH needle through the backs of the first and second stitches on the LH needle. Knit the stitches together.

Purling together through back loops
(abbreviated P2tog tbl)

This is a left-slanting decrease. When 2 stitches are purled together normally, they slant to the right on the knit side of the work. To achieve a slant to the left, insert the RH needle from the back to the front through the second stitch and then the first stitch. Purl the two stitches together.

Slipped stitch decrease – knit

(abbreviated sl, K1, psso)

This is a left-slanting decrease. Like knitting two stitches together tbl, this produces a distinct slant to the left. Instructions are: slip one, knit one, pass slipped stitch over, or sl 1, K1, psso (alternatively "skpo" or "skp").

1 Slip the first stitch on the LH needle knitwise.

2 Knit the next stitch.

3 Insert the LH needle into the slipped stitch, and lift it over the knitted stitch and off the RH needle.

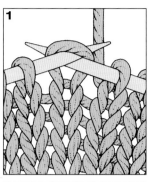

Slipped stitch decrease – purl

(abbreviated sl, P1, psso)

The instructions are: slip one, purl one, pass slipped stitch over, or sl 1, P1, psso.

1 With the yarn at the front of your work, slip the first stitch purlwise.

2 Purl the next stitch in the usual way.

3 Insert the LH needle into the slipped stitch and lift it over the purled stitch and off the RH needle to finish.

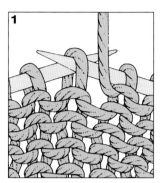

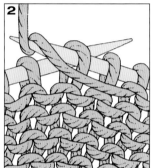

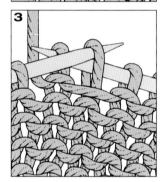

Slip, slip, knit decrease

(abbreviated ssk)

This is a left-slanting decrease. Similar to an ordinary knitwise slipped stitch decrease, this produces a smoother effect, which may be preferred in some lace patterns.

1 Slip the first stitch knitwise, then slip the second stitch knitwise.

2 Insert the LH needle into the front of the two slipped stitches, without removing them from the RH needle; knit them together through the backs of the loops with the RH needle.

Picking up stitches

You can hold stitches on a spare needle or stitch holder and work into them later, once another part of the garment is complete. Using a double-pointed or circular needle allows you to work into the stitches from either end. Your pattern will specify how many stitches to pick up, and it is important to space them evenly.

Picking up stitches on a bound-off edge

(abbreviated PU)

1 Secure the yarn just under the RH edge. Insert the needle from front to back through the first edge stitch.

2 Wrap the yarn around the needle (as if to knit) to form a loop, and draw the loop through to the front. Repeat to the end.

The first row will be worked on the wrong side.

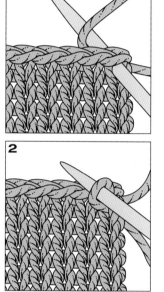

To pick up stitches on a curved edge, use large pins to mark the halfway point of the edge, then divide each of these two sections in half. Divide the number of stitches to be picked up by the number of sections, and space these groups of stitches accordingly.

Picking up stitches along a side (row-end) edge

For this method, you will probably need to plan the spacing of the stitches as for a curved edge (see below left), since working into every stitch or every other stitch may yield too many or too few stitches. Work one stitch in from the edge without encroaching on the next line of stitches.

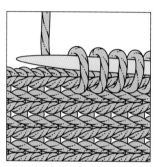

Picking up stitches with a crochet hook

1 Secure the yarn just under the LH edge. Using a crochet hook, pull a loop through to the front of the work. Insert the needle into this loop, and pull the yarn slightly to make it snug. Repeat all along the edge.

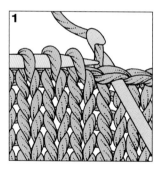

2 Left-handed knitters may prefer to work this method from the wrong side of the work, moving from right to left.

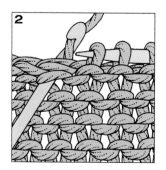

Buttonholes

Making buttonholes is an important skill to learn. There are three main types: eyelets, used on baby clothes or where small buttons are called for; horizontal, often worked in a ribbed band on the front edge of a cardigan; and vertical, which are best used decoratively, as they are the weakest of the three types.

Horizontal buttonhole

1 Work to the position for the buttonhole and bind off the specified number of stitches. Work to the end of row, or until next buttonhole is called for.

2 On the wrong side, cast on the same number of stitches as were bound off, using the single cast-on method (see page 16).

3 On the next row, work into the back of the cast-on stitches for a neat finished effect.

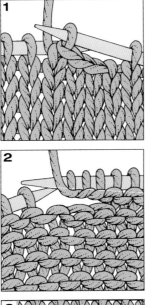

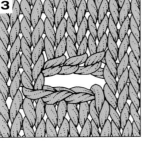

Vertical buttonhole

1 Work to the position of the buttonhole and slip the remaining stitches on to a stitch holder. Turn the work and continue for the specified number of rows, ending with a right-side row. Do not break off the yarn.

2 Join a length of yarn to the buttonhole edge of the held stitches. Using the needle in the RH stitches, work to the end, turn, and continue until there is one row less than on the RH side.

3 Fasten off the second length of yarn, and continue to the end of the row.

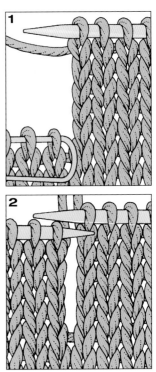

Eyelet buttonhole

1 Work to the position of the buttonhole. Yarn over (see page 30) to make a new stitch. Insert the needle knitwise into the next 2 stitches.

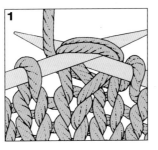

2 Knit the stitches together to decrease one stitch. Work into the new loop on the next row.

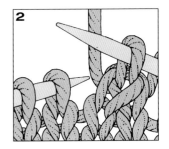

Blocking and pressing

Having spent hours knitting a garment, it is important not to skimp on the finishing process. Take care at this stage to ensure that your knitting is shown to its best advantage and that your final garment is one you can be proud of.

Equipment

Before joining pieces of knitting, you need to block them to shape, and possibly press them. Pattern instructions usually specify how to treat the various pieces. For blocking or pressing you need a firm, flat surface padded with a blanket and a sheet or towel – you can use an ironing board for small pieces. You also need rustproof pins.

Wet blocking

Pin the piece to your flat surface, right side up and following the measurements given in the pattern. Make sure that the knitting runs straight and that the shape is not distorted. Insert pins at intervals of ¾" (2 cm), at an angle through the edge stitch of the knitting into the padding. Do not pin the ribbing.

Dampen the work thoroughly with cool water, using a spray bottle. Leave the knitting to dry completely.

Steam blocking

This treatment is suitable for natural fibers only. First pin the pieces to your work surface as for wet blocking. To apply steam, use either a steam iron and a dry cloth or a dry iron and a damp cloth. Place the cloth over the work and hold the iron just above it, allowing the steam to penetrate the knitting. Allow the work to dry before removing the pins.

Pressing

Pin the pieces wrong side up to your flat surface. Do not pin the ribbing. Place the pins close together and insert them diagonally into the padded surface.

Use a steam iron and a dry cloth. For natural-synthetic blends use a dry, cool iron over a dry cloth. Do not slide the iron over the surface; instead, place it lightly on one area for a second, then lift it off. Allow the work to cool before taking it off the surface.

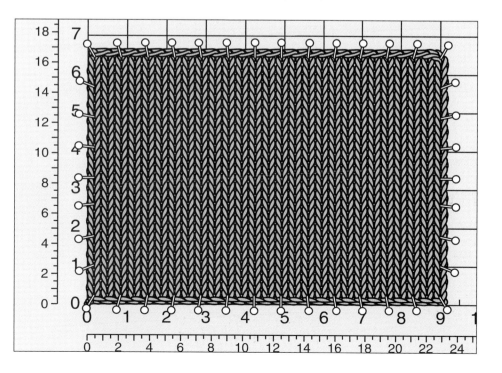

Pin the piece carefully so that the knitting runs straight.

Seams

There are several different ways of sewing pieces of knitting together, each suitable for different parts of a garment. A mattress stitch seam, for example, is ideal for joining a buttonhole band to a front edge as there is little bulk and the seam is almost invisible. Backstitch is the preferred method where strength is required – as in a side seam. You might graft some edges rather than sewing them together; for this advanced technique see page 84. You can sew a garment with the same yarn as you used for the knitting. However, if this yarn is a chunky weight, you should opt for a lighter-weight yarn, so that the seam won't be too bulky. Always secure the yarn with a couple of overcast stitches.

Mattress stitch seam

Place both pieces right side up on a flat surface.

1 Secure the yarn to the wrong side, on the RH edge, and bring it through to the right side between the edge stitch and the next stitch on the first row of knitting. Take the yarn across and under the stitch loop between the edge stitch and the next stitch on the first row on the LH edge; draw the edges together.

2 Work between the edge stitch and the next stitch on the second row on the RH edge. Continue along the seam, pulling the yarn gently to bring the two edges together smoothly.

Backstitch seam

Pin the two pieces together with right sides facing. Secure the yarn to the RH corner.

Work from right to left, taking the yarn across two stitches on the under side, then back over one stitch on top, so that the stitches meet end to end as shown. On the other side, the stitches will overlap.

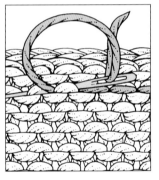

These mittens (see pages 120–123) can be finished using either a backstitch or an edge-to-edge seam.

Setting in a sleeve

You can set a sleeve with a curved sleeve head into the armhole after joining the shoulder seams and side seams of the garment and the underarm seam on the sleeve, as described here. An alternate method is to join just the shoulder seams, and then sew the sleeve cap to the garment before sewing the side and underarm seams.

1 Turn the main part of the garment wrong side out. Insert a pin into the front and back edges halfway between the shoulder and side seams. Turn the sleeve right side out and insert pins at the top center point and halfway between that pin and the underarm seam.

2 Position the sleeve inside the armhole right sides together and pin the edges together, matching the pins and seams. Add more pins around the edge, spaced about 1" (2–3 cm) apart and easing the sleeve to fit the armhole if necessary.

3 Working from the sleeve side, stitch around the armhole, about ¼" (5 mm) from the edge, using a backstitch seam.

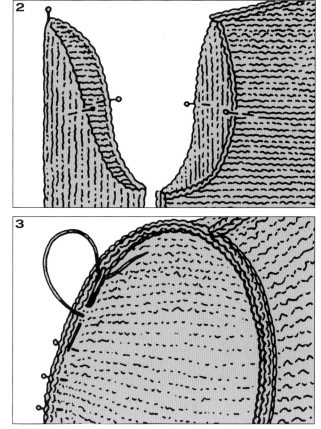

Weaving in ends

You should weave ends left from knitting or seaming into the work, usually along the edge. Use a blunt-end yarn needle to avoid splitting the stitches. Work a small stitch in the edge, then weave the yarn through the edge stitches for a short distance and cut it off. For extra security, weave it back in the opposite direction. If the yarn is too thick for the needle eye or too short to manipulate, use a crochet hook to pull it through the stitches.

Weaving in ends in a motif

When you complete a motif in intarsia knitting (see page 62), you are left with two lengths of yarn: one from the motif and one from the background. (The remaining background color is used to continue the knitting.) Cut these two ends, leaving enough for the weaving (it need not go all the way around a motif unless the difference in thickness would be visible on the right side). Weave the ends through the edge of the motif, making sure that the darker yarn does not show through the lighter knitting.

Once you have mastered the basic knitting skills and can follow a pattern, you are ready to move on to more adventurous stitch patterns. The techniques described here are more demanding, but the results are worth the effort. With a little practice you can produce gracefully coiling cables, large and small bobbles, knitted smocking and shaggy looped pile fabrics. It is worth experimenting with different yarns to see how many varied effects are possible using these stitches. For example, cables are often worked in Aran-weight yarn, as part of a traditional Aran-style sweater; but they can look beautiful in a glossy cotton or silk yarn, and also lend themselves well to mohair and angora yarns.

Special textures

Twisted stitches and cables

Some of the most beautiful stitch patterns involve crossing stitches over each other. You can cross stitches in many different ways. For example, you can work some crossing techniques entirely on the main pair of needles, where the technique is referred to as "twisting" the stitches. You can twist up to four stitches to produce mock cables that are virtually indistinguishable from those produced with a cable needle. It is important, when twisting stitches, to keep a loose tension on the yarn on the twist row as well as on those immediately preceding and following it. This makes the work easier and reduces strain on the yarn. When cabling, always use a cable needle no larger than the main needles to avoid distorting the stitches. Cables may coil to the right, called "cable back," or to the left, called "cable forward." You can work the basic cable over 4, 6, or 8 stitches.

Twisted stitches and a cable are shown in this sample. On the left, two stitches have been twisted right on every fourth row. On the right, a "cable 4 forward" has been worked on every sixth row.

Achieving cable effects

You can achieve different effects by varying the number of rows between cable twists. Working the cable every sixth row produces a graceful coil; on every fourth row, a thick, rope-like effect; on every tenth or twelfth row, a flat effect like a twisted ribbon. You can produce a novel effect by using a contrasting color for half of the cable stitches.

Variations on cabling

You can use the basic cable technique to move a single stitch or a group of stitches across the fabric, forming more complex cable and lattice patterns. The illustrations on page 42 show how to move a single knit stitch to the right or the left on a background of reverse stockinette stitch. You can use the same basic method to move different numbers of stitches at a time. To become familiar with cabling techniques, make a sample using Aran- or DK-weight yarn.

Twist 2 right
(abbreviated T2R)

1 With the RH needle, knit into the second stitch on the LH needle. Do not let the first stitch slip off the needle.

2 Knit into the first stitch on the LH needle and slip both stitches off the LH needle. On the next row, purl into the twisted stitches as usual. The stitches twist to the right.

Twist 2 right purlwise
(abbreviated T2RPW)

1 With the RH needle, purl into the second stitch on the LH needle.

2 Purl into the first stitch, then slip both stitches off the LH needle. On the next row, knit into the twisted stitches as usual. The stitches will twist to the right on the knit side of the work.

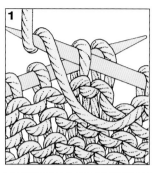

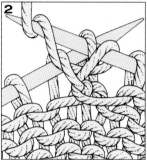

Twist 2 left
(abbreviated T2L)

1 With the RH needle behind the first stitch on the LH needle, knit into the second stitch, working through the back of the loop.

2 Knit through the back of the loop of the first stitch. On the next row, purl into the twisted stitches as usual. The stitches will now twist to the left.

Twist 2 left purlwise
(abbreviated T2LPW)

1 With the RH needle and yarn behind the first stitch on the LH needle, purl into the back of the second stitch, twisting it as shown. Take care not to let the first stitch slip off the needle.

2 Purl into the front of the first stitch and slip both stitches off the needle. On the next row, knit into the twisted stitches as usual. The stitches twist to the left on the knit side of the work.

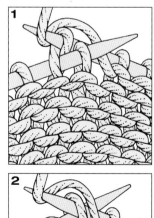

Mock cable back

This mock cable contains 4 stitches.

1 With the RH needle in front of the first 2 stitches on the LH needle, knit the third stitch, and then knit the fourth stitch. Leave all 4 stitches on the LH needle.

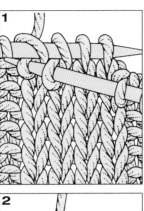

2 Now knit the second stitch and then the first stitch on the LH needle and slip all 4 stitches off the needle. On the following row, purl these stitches, remembering to keep the yarn tension fairly loose. The resulting cable will twist to the right.

Mock cable forward

For this mock cable, knit the third and fourth stitches through the back of the loops. Then knit the first stitch through the front in the usual way, slip it off the needle, knit the second stitch through the front, and slip all stitches off the needle. The resulting cable twists to the left.

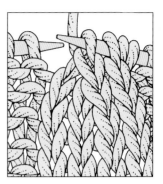

Cross 2 back

(abbreviated Cr2B)

1 Slip the purl stitch immediately before the knit stitch on to a cable needle and hold it at the back of the work. Knit the knit stitch.

2 Purl the stitch from the cable needle.

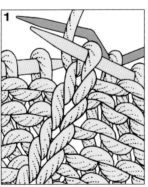

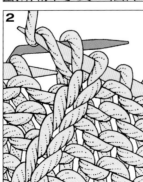

Cross 2 forward

(abbreviated Cr2F)

1 Slip the knit stitch on to the cable needle and hold it at the front of the work. Purl the next purl stitch.

2 Knit the stitch from the cable needle.

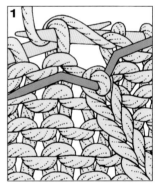

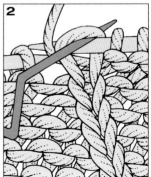

Cable 6 back
(abbreviated C6B)

1 Work to the position of the cable, slip the next 3 stitches onto the cable needle and hold them at the back of the work. Knit the next 3 stitches.

2 Knit the 3 stitches from the cable needle. On the next row, purl these stitches as usual. The cable coils to the right.

Cable 6 forward
(abbreviated C6F)

1 Work to the position of the cable, slip the next 3 stitches onto the cable needle and hold them at the front of the work. Knit the next 3 stitches.

2 Knit the 3 stitches from the cable needle. On the next row, purl these stitches as usual. The cable coils to the left.

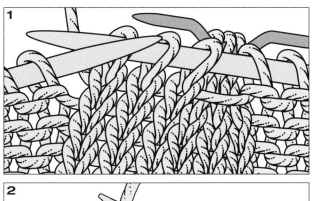

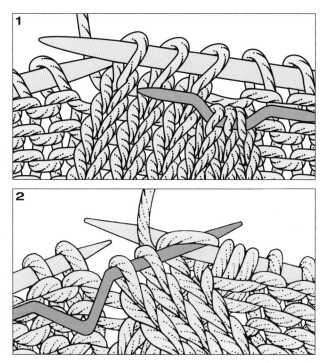

The Single Cable Pullover on page 128 features a prominent single cable, ideal for a beginner.

Bobbles and knots

Different sizes and shapes of bobbles can be made by making several stitches out of one stitch and then decreasing back to a single stitch, after working one or more rows on only the increased stitches. You usually work the extra rows on the bobble stitches alone, which makes the bobble stand out from the background, as it is attached to the rest of the knitting only at the top and bottom. Small bobbles, or knots, are made by decreasing the increased stitches, all in the same row of knitting.

Bobble – method 1

This bobble is worked in reverse stockinette stitch and is shown on a stockinette stitch fabric. For a stockinette stitch bobble, reverse the "knit" and "purl" instructions in steps 2 and 3.

1 On a right-side row, knit, purl, knit, and purl into the same stitch, thus making 4 stitches out of 1. Turn the work.

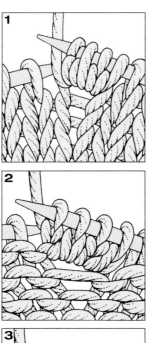

2 Knit these 4 stitches. Turn. Purl the stitches. Turn again.

3 Repeat step 2 once more. The right (purl) side of the bobble is now facing.

4 Working from left to right, use the LH needle to lift the second, third and fourth stitches over the first, thus decreasing back to one stitch and completing the bobble.

Bobble – method 2

This bobble is slightly flatter than that shown in method 1.

1 Knit 1, yarn over, knit 1, yarn over, knit 1. Turn. Purl the stitches and yarn overs. Turn again.

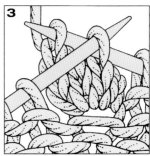

2 Knit the 5 stitches. Turn. Purl 2 together, purl 1, purl 2 together: 3 stitches. Turn.

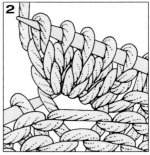

3 Slip 1, knit 2 together, then pass the slipped stitch over to complete the bobble.

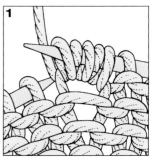

Knot – method 1

This small bobble, or knot, is produced in essentially the same way as the method 1 bobble opposite, but the increased stitches are immediately decreased.

1 Knit, purl, knit, purl, and knit into the stitch, making a total of 5 stitches out of 1.

2 With the LH needle, lift the second, third, fourth and fifth stitches over the first one, decreasing back to 1 stitch and completing the knot.

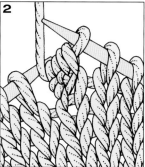

Knot – method 2

This method produces a slightly flatter and smoother knot than method 1, left.

1 Knit into the front, back, front, and back of the stitch, making 4 stitches out of 1. With the LH needle, lift the second stitch over the first stitch.

2 Lift the third and fourth stitches over the first stitch, completing the knot.

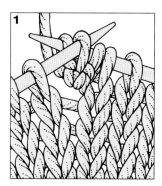

Contrasting bobbles and knots

To work a bobble or knot in a contrasting color, simply tie the new color to the first color at the position for the bobble on the wrong side of the work, drop the first color and work the bobble in the new color. When the bobble is completed, break off the yarn and tie the ends together securely. When the knitting is completed, weave the ends into the wrong side with a darning or tapestry needle. If working a series of bobbles across a row at short intervals, you may prefer to weave in the contrasting yarn as you go (as shown on page 65) so that you won't have so many yarn ends to weave in later.

You can work bobbles in as many different colors as you like.

Wrapping techniques

A variety of effects can be achieved by manipulating the yarn in different ways – wrapping it around your thumb to make a looped-pile fabric; wrapping it around a group of stitches to draw them together and produce smocking; and wrapping it around the needle two or more times to create a line or area of openwork called a dropped-stitch pattern.

Loop stitch

It is possible to produce looped pile or shaggy fabrics in knitting by winding the yarn around the thumb at regular close intervals. You can leave the resulting loops as they are, or you can cut them for a shaggy effect. A loop stitch is easier to work if you hold the yarn in your right hand, as shown on page 18.

Working loop stitch

Begin by working 2 rows of stockinette stitch, then knit 1 or 2 stitches for the selvage.

1 Knit the next stitch, but do not let the original stitch slip off the needle. Bring the yarn forward between the needles and wrap it around the left thumb from back to front, making a loop of the desired length. The length of the loop can be increased by holding the thumb lower.

2 Knit again into the same stitch, and slip the original stitch off the LH needle, still keeping the thumb in the loop.

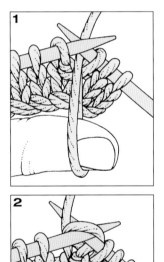

3 With the thumb still in the loop, insert the LH needle through the front of the 2 stitches just made, and knit both stitches together through the back. Slip the thumb out of the loop. Work to the position of the next loop, and repeat steps 1–3. (In the drawing below the loops are shown separated by a single knit stitch. They may be more widely spaced if desired.)

4 Purl the next row. Slip the free needle through the loops, and pull them gently downward before continuing the knitting.

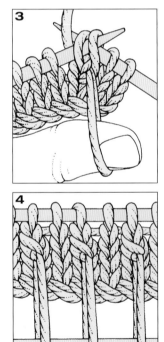

Smocking

You can produce a smocked fabric either by sewing a knitted fabric in a pattern (see page 72) or by knitting in the smocking as you go. The latter method, shown here, is based on a rib pattern, which you can vary by adjusting the thickness and/or spacing of the ribs.

Use a cable needle to group stitches together so that they can be wrapped with the yarn. You can wrap the grouped stitches before working them, as shown here, or you can work them first and then wrap them.

Basic ribbed smocking

Cast on a multiple of 8 stitches plus 10. Work in K2, P2 rib for 5 rows. On the 6th row (right side), work the smocking, as follows:

1 Purl the first 2 (purl) stitches. Slip the next 6 stitches onto the cable needle; hold them at front. Now wind the yarn twice around these stitches from left to right, pulling it firmly.

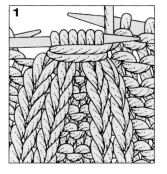

2 Knit 2, purl 2, knit 2 from the cable needle.

3 Repeat steps 1 and 2 to the end of the row.

4 Work in rib for 5 rows.

5 On the 12th row purl the first 2 stitches. Slip 2 knit stitches on to the cable needle. Wind the yarn around these stitches twice, knit them, then slip them off the cable needle. Purl 2 stitches, repeat steps 2–4 to the last 2 stitches; knit 2. These 12 rows form the pattern.

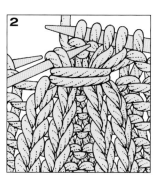

Dropped-stitch patterns

The technique shown here consists of elongating stitches to produce an open, ladder-like effect, either across the whole row or in small areas throughout the fabric. The yarn may be wrapped two or more times around the needle. This technique can be used as the basis of more elaborate patterns, such as elongated cross stitch.

Basic elongated stitch

1 Insert the RH needle knitwise into the stitch, wrap the yarn twice around the needle, and draw the 2 loops through the stitch, allowing it to slip off the needle. Repeat this step to the end of the row.

2 On the following row, purl into the first of each pair of loops and allow the extra loop to drop off the needle. You can use either side of the work as the right side. Produce longer stitches by winding the yarn 3 or more times around the needle.

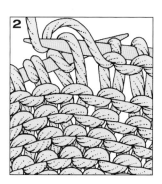

By now you will be confident in knitting back and forth in rows to produce flat pieces of knitted fabric, which you then join to make a garment. Now let's look at the technique of knitting in the round to produce a seamless fabric – either tubular or flat. You can use tubular fabrics in many ways: for ribbing around necklines; for socks, gloves and hats; and sometimes for the main body of a sweater. You can sew flat medallion shapes together to make a scarf, shawl, tablecloth, or bedspread, or use a large medallion to make a cushion cover or a shawl.

Knitting in the round

Working in the round

Using circular and double-pointed needles lets you achieve many different fabrics and finishing details that would be less satisfactory or even impossible if worked on conventional straight needles. By working in rounds on these needles, you can make a seamless, tubular fabric, to form the main part of a pullover, or a turtleneck collar; you can make leggings or socks, as well as berets and shawls.

Some knitting in the round is best done on a circular needle, some with double-pointed needles; some can be done with either. Whichever kind you are using, there are several points to remember. First of all, it is important to keep track of the beginning of each round. To do this, place a ring marker or a loop of contrasting yarn at the beginning of the round, and slip it onto the right-hand needle as you begin each new round. It may also be necessary to mark certain shaping points of pattern repeats in the same way.

When picking up stitches for working in the round–at a neckline, for example – the pattern will specify the correct number for the stitch pattern repeat. However, if you are altering a pattern in which this section is knitted flat, you may need to adjust the number of stitches to make sure you have an exact multiple of the repeat. For example, if you are working a K2, P2 rib, the total number of stitches must be divisible by 4; otherwise, the stitch pattern will not join up correctly.

Knitting with a circular needle

Of the two kinds of needle used for knitting in the round, the circular needle is easier to use. Only two needle points are involved in the work, and the bulk of the knitting slides easily between them as the work progresses. Also, there is only one join, as opposed to three or more if you are using double-pointed needles, which makes it easier to produce a smooth fabric. However, the circular needle cannot be used for small items, because the knitting needs to reach from one point of the needle to the other without stretching. The length of the needle used should be at least 2" (5 cm) less than the circumference of the piece of knitting.

If you have never used a circular needle, it's a good idea to practice using one for working back and forth in rows, as explained at right. Some people prefer them to straight needles. And if you're knitting on a train or bus, they are less obtrusive to your seat companions. If you're changing from one kind of needle to the other, make sure your tension remains the same.

Before beginning to work with a new circular needle or one that has been coiled up in its package for some time, straighten it by soaking it for about 15 minutes in warm water then pulling it gently through your fingers.

Working in rows with a circular needle

A circular needle is useful for working back and forth in rows. The weight of the work is distributed equally along the cable needle, which is ideal for large, heavy pieces, that can be tiring to work on a pair of ordinary needles.

To use a circular needle in this way, cast on in the chosen method, but do not join the stitches. Work the first row beginning with the last cast-on stitch. At the end of the row, turn the needle so that the point with the last-worked stitch is in your left hand, and work the next row.

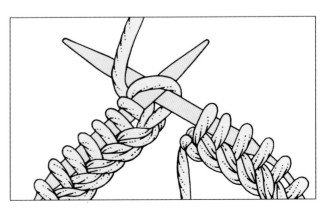

Tubular knitting on a circular needle

1 Cast on the required number of stitches. If you are using a single-needle method of casting on, wind an elastic band around one end of the needle to prevent the stitches from slipping off. Before beginning to knit, make sure that the stitches reach easily from one point to the other. Hold the needle so that the end with the last cast-on stitch is in your right hand and the end with the first cast-on stitch is in your left hand. Make sure that the stitches are not twisted on the needle; their lower edges should lie towards the center of the ring. Place a ring marker or a loop of contrasting yarn over the RH point, and insert the point into the first stitch on the LH needle.

2 Work the first stitch, pulling the yarn firmly to prevent a gap at the join. Work the first (right-side) round of the specified pattern around to the marker. Slip the marker to the RH needle and continue with the second round of the pattern. Continue working in the chosen pattern, noting that all rounds are right side.

3 Bind off in the usual way. After drawing the yarn through the last stitch, take it through the first stitch of the round.

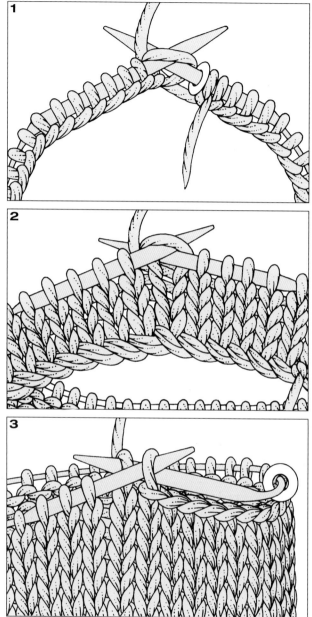

These Super Socks (page 142) are worked on double-pointed needles (see page 52).

Knitting with double-pointed needles

Double-pointed needles are sold in sets of four or five needles all of the same size. A set of four is shown in these illustrations, but the principle is the same when using five. These needles are most often used for tubular knitting where there are too few stitches for even the shortest circular needle, such as a seamless turtleneck collar on a sweater. The pattern may specify how many stitches are to be picked up; if not, you can either divide the number of stitches evenly or base the division on the shape of the work. For example, you might divide a V-neck into right front, left front and back, with a needle for each. The basic technique of picking up the stitches is the same as shown on page 33.

TIP

When resuming work on a piece of knitting on double-pointed needles, undo two or three stitches and work them again. They will have stretched slightly, and the interruption might be noticeable. The same applies to knitting worked in rows on ordinary needles, if you have had to stop in the middle of a row.

Tubular knitting on double-pointed needles

1 Begin by casting the required number of stitches onto a single-pointed needle of the same size as the double-pointed needles. Slip the stitches onto the double-pointed needles, leaving one needle free for working the stitches. Here, three needles out of a set of four are used.

2 Arrange the needles so that their points cross as shown. Check to make sure that the stitches are not twisted. Place a ring marker over the point holding the last cast-on stitch. With the remaining needle, knit the first cast-on stitch, pulling the yarn firmly to close the gap.

3 Continue working into all the stitches on the first needle. When this needle is free, use it to work the stitches on the second needle. Continue in this way, taking care to pull the yarn firmly when working the first stitch on each needle and slipping the marker at the beginning of each new round. When the work is the required length, bind off as usual. Draw the yarn through the first stitch of the round to make a neat join.

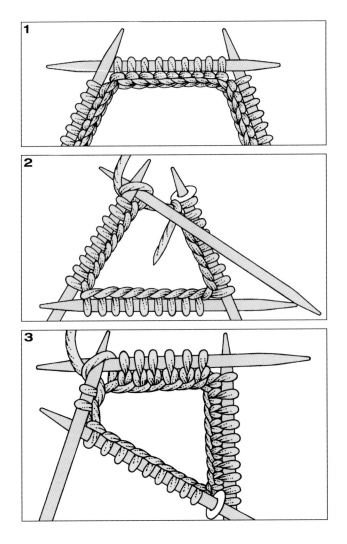

Medallions

By working in rounds, and increasing in a regular sequence, it's possible to make a variety of medallion shapes, useful for everything from scarves to throws. Using double-pointed needles, you work from the center outward (it is also possible to work from the outer edge inward, decreasing rather than increasing). If you work the increases at the same point on every round, they form a pattern of straight lines radiating out from the center. If you change their placement, you produce a swirl pattern. The type of increase you work also affects the appearance of the medallions. Bar increases produce an embossed effect, while make 1 and lifted increases produce a more subtle pattern (see pages 28–29). For a decorative effect, use an openwork (YO) increase.

Crocheted foundation

You may find this method of beginning a medallion easier than the cast-on method, especially where there are only 8 stitches in the first round.

Crochet a chain (see page 77) consisting of 8 stitches. Join the first and last chain with a slip stitch. Pick up 1 stitch through each chain (drawing the first loop through the chain and the loop that was on the hook as shown). Insert the needle through the top of each chain as shown. Place 2 stitches on each of the four double-pointed needles.

Working a square medallion

Cast on 8 stitches to a double-pointed needle using the cable method (see page 16).

1 Arrange the stitches on 4 needles, as shown, and tie a thread marker at the beginning of the round – just before the last cast-on stitch.

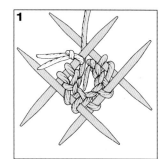

2 Round 1: Using the fifth needle, knit into the back of every stitch.
Round 2: Knit into the front and back of every stitch: 16 stitches on the needles.

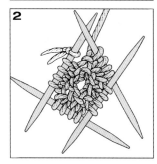

3 Round 3: Knit all stitches in the normal way. **Round 4:** Knit into the front and back of the first stitch, knit 1, knit into the front and back of the third stitch, knit 1. Repeat on the remaining three sets of 4 stitches: 24 stitches. Placing each increase bar one stitch in from the corner, repeat rounds 3 and 4 until the medallion is the desired size. Bind off.

Turning a heel

Socks are nearly always worked in the round, on double-pointed needles, in order to avoid the discomfort of a seam. The only complicated shaping involved is turning the heel, but even this is less difficult than it first appears. There are several basic methods of turning a heel; the one described here is called a Dutch heel. The shaping involves a technique known as short-row shaping, in which you hold some stitches on the needle while working others. In turning a heel you gradually decrease the number of held stitches and incorporate them into the center section of the heel. You then rejoin the heel to the instep stitches. The main part of a sock is normally worked in stockinette stitch, while the leg and cuff are generally worked in some sort of rib pattern. Take care to cast on loosely so that the edge will not be uncomfortably tight.

1 Using a set of 4 double-pointed needles, cast on the specified number of stitches for the sock. (The number is generally divisible by 3.) Work in single rib (or other rib pattern) for the required length down to the top of the heel. Break off the yarn.

2 Divide the heel stitches from those that will be used for the instep. The respective numbers will vary according to the pattern and the size. Slip the first half and the last half of the stitches in the round onto one double-pointed needle. Slip the remaining instep stitches on to a spare needle; a short circular needle is convenient for this, as it holds the stitches in a curve, out of the way.

3 Rejoin the yarn to the RH edge of the heel stitches. Work back and forth in rows in stockinette stitch until the heel is the required depth from ankle to bottom of heel, ending with a purl row.

4 On the next row, work across the specified number of stitches (the number will vary with the pattern, but should be approximately two thirds of the total), then decrease 1 stitch as follows: sl 1, K1, psso. Turn, leaving the remaining stitches unworked.

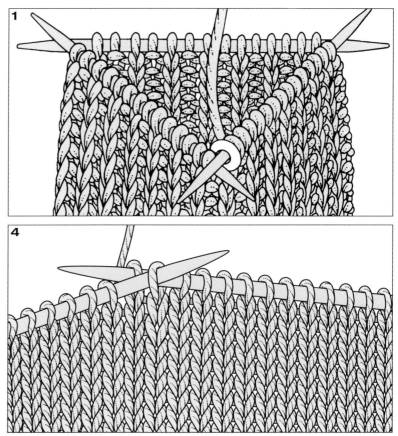

5 Purl across the first half of the stitches, then decrease 1 stitch: P2tog. Turn, leaving the remaining stitches unworked. Continue working on the center stitches; at the end of every row work in 1 of the held stitches, at the same time decreasing 1 stitch. On knit rows decrease as in step 4; on purl rows, decrease as in step 5. Continue in this way until all the held stitches have been decreased, ending with a wrong-side row.

6 Resume working in rounds on the 3 double-pointed needles. Work across the heel stitches, then pick up and knit the specified number along the left side of the heel;. Using a second needle, work across the instep stitches. Using a third needle, pick up the specified number of stitches along the right side of the heel, then knit across half of the heel stitches. Place a marker at this point to indicate the beginning of the round.

7 Work one round even. Begin to decrease the stitches on either side of the instep: work to the last 3 stitches on the first needle, K2tog, work across the instep stitches, work the first stitch on third needle, then sl 1, K1, psso, work to the end of round.

8 Repeat this decrease round until the specified number of stitches remain on the needles. The sock is then worked even until the toe shaping.

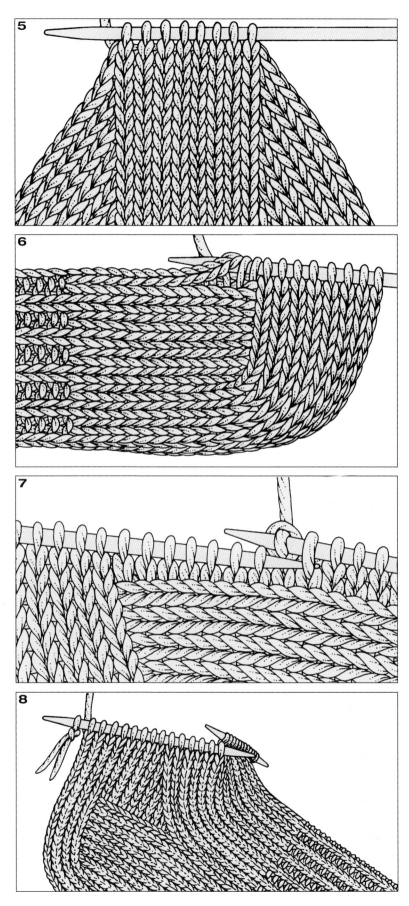

Shaping a gusset

A traditional Guernsey sweater is knitted mainly in the round. Even the sleeves are worked in this way, on stitches picked up from the yoke. The shaping incorporates an underarm gusset, which helps to make the garment comfortable. Although a gusset can be worked separately and sewn in, it is not difficult to knit one in as shown here, while working in the round. The garment is worked in the round up to the armpit. To indicate the side "seams," purl a single stitch at these points on each round. At the widest part of the gusset the circular knitting is interrupted and the front and back completed separately, working back and forth in rows. Then stitches are picked up for the sleeves and the circular knitting is begun again. The gusset stitches are decreased down to a single purled stitch for the underarm sleeve "seam."

1 To begin shaping the gusset, increase 1 stitch on either side of the "seam" by working a make 1 increase (see page 29) just before the purled stitch, knitting the stitch, then increasing again just after it. Work the next round even.

2 On the next round, work up to the 3 gusset stitches, make 1, work across gusset, make 1. Continue in this way, adding 2 stitches to the gusset on alternate rounds, until the gusset is the desired width. Work one round even; slip the gusset stitches on to a stitch holder.

3 Complete the front and back sections separately. Join the shoulder seams.

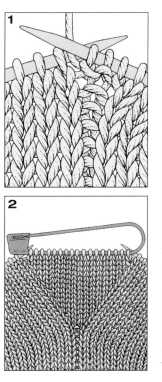

4 Using a set of double-pointed needles, knit across the gusset stitches, then pick up and knit the stitches for the sleeve from the front and back of the garment.

5 Work the sleeve from the top down, decreasing on either side of the gusset. On the first round: sl 1, K1, psso, knit to last 2 gusset sts, K2tog. Work the next round without decreasing.

6 Continue to decrease 2 stitches on alternate rounds until 1 stitch remains in the gusset. This stitch marks the sleeve "seam;" purl it on every round.

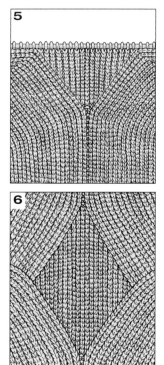

Joining in new yarn

You can avoid joining in yarn mid-row when working back and forth, but when knitting in the round, joining at the end of a row isn't an option. Join in at an inconspicuous place, such as at the underarm of a sweater.

Double strand method

Use this method if the yarn is fuzzy and the stitch pattern is a textured one. The first stitch in the new yarn should be a knit stitch.

1 Having worked the last stitch in the old yarn, let this yarn drop down on the wrong side of the work. Turn back the end of the new yarn for 4" (10 cm). Insert the needle into the next stitch and draw through the loop of the new yarn to form the first stitch in the new yarn.

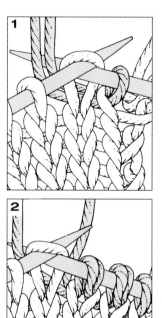

2 Work the next two or three stitches in the double strand, then let the short end of the new yarn drop. On the following round, treat each pair of double strands as one stitch. Trim the short end of new yarn close to the work. Weave the old yarn into the wrong side (see page 37).

Threading-in method

This method is preferred when working stockinette stitch in a smooth yarn. Using a darning needle, thread the end of the new yarn through the old yarn for about 1½" (4 cm). Continue knitting, and work in the joined yarn. Trim the loose ends later.

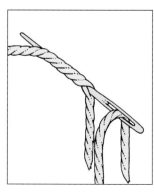

Stitch patterns in the round

Instructions for stitch patterns are normally given for working in rows. This might put you off working in the round, thinking that you will be able to use only the basic stitches.

Happily, however, you can easily convert many stitch patterns for working in the round. As already noted (see page 50), you produce stockinette stitch by knitting every round. Conversely, reverse stockinette stitch results if your purl every round. For garter stitch, you knit and purl alternate rounds. For most rib patterns, you simply knit and purl the same stitches on every round. The principle, therefore, is that any stitch you normally purl on a wrong-side row should now be knitted when you work on the right side, and vice versa.

This means that any stitch pattern in which you simply purl every wrong-side row can easily be worked in the round by knitting all these rounds.

If you wish to use a more complex stitch pattern, you may first need to work a sample in rows, until you become familiar with its construction. Then write your own revised instructions and work a sample in the round. However, when working in the round, remember to omit any edge selvage stitches.

Try working this simple stitch in rounds (see page 168).

There are many ways of combining two or more colors in a piece of knitting – some complex, some extremely simple – all capable of producing rich and exciting effects. They include simple horizontal stripes, fascinating slipstitch patterns, jacquard motifs, and traditional Fair Isle designs. Many patterns include colorwork; but it is also possible to add a color pattern to a one-color design, thereby giving it your own personal stamp of individuality.

Colorwork

Horizontal stripes

You can create many effects simply by working rows in different colors to produce stripes. The simplest version is a two-color stripe, where you change the colors after a specified number of rows. Worked in stockinette stitch, stripes create a neat, crisp appearance. You can achieve more subtle effects by using shades of the same color; by varying the number of rows worked in a regular or random pattern; by using the purled side of the work thereby giving the color changes a broken appearance; or by introducing the occasional purled row on the right side of a stockinette stitch fabric for textural interest. Stripes knit horizontally need not run horizontally. If you work the garment from one side edge to the other the stripes will run vertically. (You can achieve true vertical stripes by using one of the methods shown on pages 62–63.)

Joining new colors

1 Tie the new color to the old one at the RH edge of the work, using a double knot. Do not cut off the old yarn.

2 Continue knitting with the new yarn. On every second row twist the two yarns around each other to help keep the edge neat. When changing back to the first color, bring it in front of the second color. Avoid pulling the yarn tightly when beginning to knit with the new yarn.

If the yarn is fine, up to three colors can be carried up the side in this way. Where more colors are used, or where one color is not used for many rows, it's better to cut them off and rejoin as required. This is also necessary, of course, where new colors are introduced on wrong-side rows and joined at the LH edge.

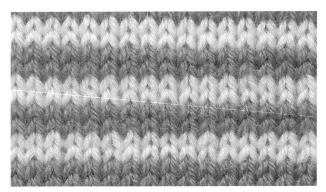

You can work horizontal stripes simply by changing color at the side edge. Here the colors have been changed after every two rows.

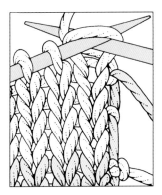

Chevron stripes are created by working a chevron stitch pattern and changing color as for ordinary horizontal stripes.

Slipstitch color patterns

Slipstitch color patterns are knit using one color per row. You achieve a blended color effect by slipping stitches, so that the color from the previous row encroaches upon the row being worked. The working yarn is loosely carried behind the slipped stitches. In some patterns the stitches may draw in, so it's important to make a good-sized gauge swatch if you substitute a slipstitch pattern for another stitch. The stitches slipped in these patterns are always slipped purlwise. Instructions "with yarn at front" and "with yarn at back" refer to the back and front in relation to the knitter; not to the right and wrong sides of the work. You take the yarn directly to the front or back and not over the needle. Having slipped the stitches, the yarn is at the back of the work if the next stitch is a knit stitch or at the front if it is a purl stitch.

Basic slipstitch technique

The simple pattern shown here – called tricolor wave stripe – will introduce you to the principles of working slipstitch color patterns.

1 Cast on a multiple of 4 stitches plus 1, using color A.
Row 1 Purl one row.
Row 2 (RS) With color B, K1, *with yarn at back sl 3 purlwise, K1, rep from * to end.

2 Row 3 With yarn B, P2, *with yarn at front sl 1, P3, rep from * to last 3 sts, sl 1, P2.
Row 4 With B, knit to end.
Row 5 With B, purl to end.
Rows 6–9 With C, rep rows 2–5.
Rows 10–13 With A, rep rows 2–5.

The right side of the tricolor wave stripe illustrates the construction of a typical slipstitch color pattern.

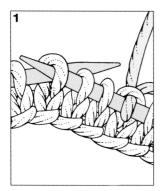
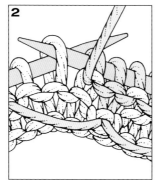

The reverse side of the tricolor wave stripe demonstrates how yarn is carried from one stitch to another.

Vertical color changes

You can work patterns with more than one color in a row using one of several methods: carrying, or "stranding," the unused color loosely along the back of the work until it is needed again; "weaving" the unused yarn into the work at intervals, until it is needed; and working with several different balls of yarn, positioned across the work and picked up as required – a method called "intarsia." The method you choose is often dictated by the type of design, but also by the weight and color of the yarn you are using. For example, you would normally knit a repeating-motif pattern, such as a Fair Isle design that uses only two colors in any one row, using the stranding method and then incorporating weaving where the unused yarn must span long distances. Weaving is better suited to busy patterns.

Intarsia

Intarisa might be used for a design that includes more than two colors in a row, because carrying more than two colors across every row would make the work too bulky. Intarsia is also the best choice for designs with wide vertical or diagonal stripes, with 10 or more stitches in each stripe. Using the stranding method would leave long strands of yarn on the wrong side, which are likely to be snagged. Weaving in the yarn might leave noticeable marks on the right side. Intarsia is also good for working large repeating motifs, individual motifs, and pictorial knitting.

The first step is to prepare the yarn by winding it onto bobbins. Yarn on bobbins doesn't unroll as balls of yarn do, so they are less likely to become tangled. You can buy plastic bobbins at some yarn shops; however, if the yarn you are using is thick, you may prefer to make your own bobbins from pieces of cardboard as shown in the box, right.

Motifs designed to be worked using intarsia can sometimes be more easily worked in duplicate stitch (see page 70).

In the illustrations, opposite, the fabric being worked is stockinette stitch; in the case of reverse stockinette stitch you hold the yarns on the knit side of the work. The process of twisting the yarns is essentially the same: bring the old yarn over the new yarn, then bring it up in the correct position to work the next stitch.

Making a bobbin

Cut a cardboard rectangle of the desired size. For thick yarns, about 2" x 3½" (5 cm x 8 cm) will do. In each short end, cut notches as shown. Wind the yarn through the notches.

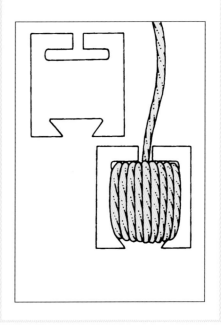

Changing color on a knit row

Work in the first color to the point for the color change. If the second color is being introduced for the first time, tie it to the first color. On subsequent rows the procedure is as follows:

Drop the first color over the second, pick up the second color and continue knitting with it. In this way, the yarns are twisted around each other. If this were not done, the two areas of color would be separate, leaving a split in the fabric.

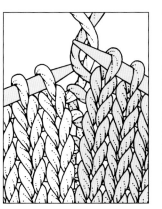

Changing color on a purl row

Work in the first color to the point for the color change. Drop the first color over the second, pick up the second color and continue purling with it. On both knit and purl rows, work the stitches before and after the color change fairly tightly to avoid leaving a gap.

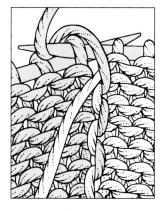

The wrong side of intarsia work shows how the two colors twist around each other where they are joined together.

Stranding yarns

Stranding is the basic technique used when knitting a repeating motif using two colors that are alternated at short intervals. As a general rule you should not strand yarns across more than five stitches; otherwise the elasticity of the work is likely to be impaired. Where you must carry yarn for more than five stitches, you should weave it into the work, using the technique shown on page 65. Both stranding and weaving are easier to do on knit rows than on purl rows, making them perfect for knitting in the round. Whether you work in rounds or in rows, it is important to hold the unused yarn loosely in order to avoid puckering the fabric. For a smooth fabric it is best to hold one yarn in each hand as you knit.

Stranding yarn on a knit row

1 On the row in which the second color is introduced, join it at the RH edge. Begin knitting in the color specified by the pattern, carrying the other color loosely across the back of the work. To knit with the RH yarn, hold the LH yarn slightly below the needles.

2 To knit with the LH yarn, hold the RH yarn out of the way.

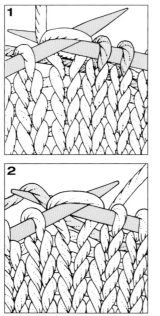

Stranding yarn on a purl row

Here the process is the same as for a knit row except that the stranded yarn is held at the front of the work.

1 To purl with the RH yarn, hold the LH yarn under the needles.

2 To purl with the LH yarn, hold the RH yarn out of the way.

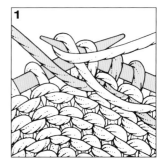

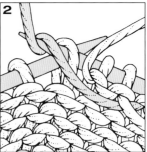

The best way of working an Argyle pattern is to hold one yarn in each hand, as shown, and then knit with them alternately, stranding or weaving the unused color on the wrong side of the work.

Weaving yarns

In weaving, you occasionally catch unused yarn into a stitch. You can do this on every other stitch to produce a dense fabric with no loose strands on the wrong side, or you can do it every few stitches. Avoid working the yarn into stitches directly above one another, as this may cause a visible indentation in the fabric.

Weaving in LH yarn on a knit row

When knitting with the RH yarn, bring the LH yarn alternately below and above the stitches.

To weave the LH yarn below, simply hold it under the work as if for stranding (see page 64).

To weave the LH yarn above, bring it over the RH needle. Use the RH yarn to knit as usual; draw this loop through the stitch.

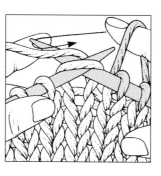

Weaving in LH yarn on a purl row

When purling with the RH yarn, take the LH yarn alternately below and above the stitches.

To weave the LH yarn below, simply hold it away from the work as if for stranding (see page 64).

To weave the LH yarn above, take it over the RH needle (but not all the way around it), and purl with the RH yarn.

Weaving in RH yarn on a knit row

To weave the RH yarn above, simply hold it away from the work as if for stranding and knit with the LH yarn. To take the RH yarn below:

1 Bring the RH yarn around the needle as if to knit.

2 Bring the LH yarn around the needle as if to knit.

3 Reverse the RH yarn, taking it to the left and under the needle point and thus off the needle.

4 Complete the stitch in the LH yarn.

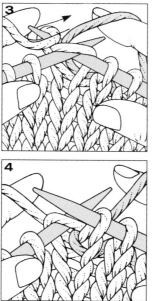

Weaving in RH yarn on a purl row

To weave the RH yarn above, simply hold it away from the work as if for stranding and purl with the LH yarn. To weave the RH yarn below:

1 Loop the RH yarn around the needle as shown.

2 Bring the LH yarn over the needle as if to purl.

3 Reverse the RH yarn, taking it to the left and under the needle point and thus off the needle.

4 Complete the stitch in the LH yarn.

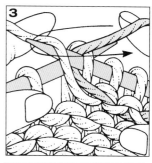

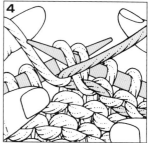

Following a chart

Individual and repeating motifs for color patterns are often given in the form of a chart, which is easier to follow than written instructions. The colors may be shown on the chart, or they may be represented by symbols, with an accompanying key. Each square on the chart represents a single stitch. You work a chart from bottom to top. Right-side rows are normally given odd numbers, and are worked from right to left. You work the even-numbered, wrong-side rows from left to right. This rule does not apply to working in the round (see page 50) in which you knit all the rounds from right to left. Charts for repeating motifs normally include only the one repeat, along with any edge stitches required. The repeat itself is marked off with a heavy line; for patterns in multiple sizes there may be additional edge stitches given for the larger sizes.

Intarsia chart

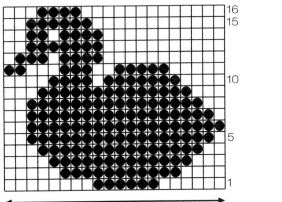

Motif worked over 20 stitches.

Key

□ A

● B

The simple chart above is for an individual duck motif. Only one contrasting color is used, represented by a dot. Only every fifth row is marked on the chart, plus the final 16th row.

Fair Isle chart

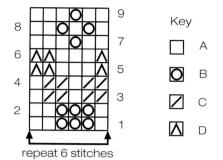

repeat 6 stitches

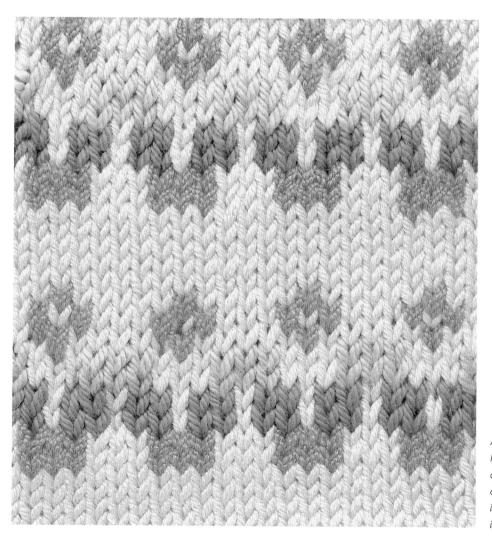

A slightly more complicated Fair Isle pattern uses a main color and three contrasting colors. Every row on the chart is marked. The pattern repeat is worked over 6 stitches.

TIP

When following a chart, it is important to keep careful track of your progress. A good way of doing this is to photocopy the chart and draw a line through each row as you complete it. If the chart is small, enlarging it when you photocopy it will make it easier to follow.

Knitting is often embellished in some way. There may be a twisted cord around a waistline or at a neck, or the front opening of a cardigan might have a crocheted edging. Perhaps you will work beads, sequins, or embroidery stitches into your knitting, or add a deep fringe to a shawl to help it hang gracefully. Conversely, you can use knitting itself as the embellishment, in the form of a lacy knitted edging. On the following few pages you will find instructions for all of these techniques.

Embellishments

Embroidery on knitting

You can use embroidery stitches to add motifs to a piece of plain knitting or to enhance or accentuate a stitch pattern. The most common embroidery technique used in knitting is duplicate stitch, also known as Swiss darning. The embroidery is worked on stockinette stitch fabric and gives the appearance of having been knitted in. Motifs for duplicate stitch are normally given in chart form, with one square of the chart representing each stitch. You can also use a cross-stitch technique in the same way. Embroidery on knitting is always worked with a blunt-end yarn needle to avoid splitting the yarn. You can use a knitting yarn or embroidery thread; just make sure that the thread is appropriate in weight and texture for the background and the technique used. It is important to stitch with an easy tension to preserve the elasticity of the fabric.

Duplicate stitch

Use a single strand of yarn, the same weight and type as that used for the knitting. Begin at the bottom RH corner of the motif, and secure the yarn with one or two stitches on the wrong side of the area to be covered with the embroidery. Bring the needle up through the base of the first stitch to be embroidered.

1 Take the needle up to the right, along over the stitch, then under it from right to left, bringing it out as shown in the upper left of the drawing.

2 Take the needle down at the center of the stitch, where it emerged, and then one stitch to the left as shown in the lower left of the drawing. Repeat steps 1 and 2 to cover this and all subsequent stitches. Take care not to pull the stitches too tightly.

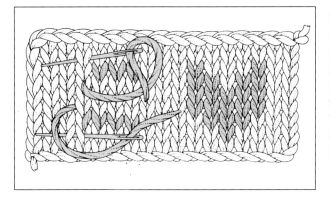

Cross stitch

This stitch is also well suited to stockinette stitch fabric. The yarn used should be somewhat thinner than that used for the knitting. Depending on the scale of the work, it is best to work over groups of four stitches. Secure the yarn to the wrong side.

1 Bring the needle up at the lower RH corner of the area to be covered with the stitch, and take it down at the upper LH.

2 Bring it up at the lower LH corner and take it back down at the upper RH corner to complete the stitch.

3 When working cross stitch it is important that all the lower stitches slant in the same direction and all the top stitches slant in the other direction. Therefore, it is better to work rows of cross stitch in two stages.

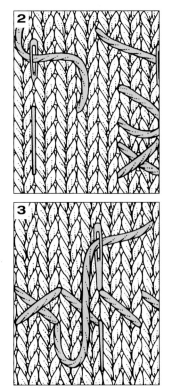

Chain stitch

You can use this versatile stitch to work lines in any direction. Varying the thickness of yarn and the spacing of stitches produces quite different effects.

1 Bring the needle up to the right side of the work, form the thread into a small loop, and take the needle back down into the fabric and up inside the loop (top). Pull the thread gently to tighten the loop. Continue forming loops in this way along the line of stitching. Secure the last loop by taking the needle down into the fabric just outside the loop (bottom).

2 You can work individual chain stitches in a circle to suggest the petals of a flower; in this form the stitch is called lazy daisy. You can also scatter loops over the surface.

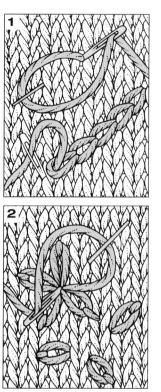

French knots

It is usually better to choose a yarn at least as thick as that used for the knitting, so that the knots will stand out prominently on the surface.

Bring the needle up at the point for the knot. Then, holding the yarn taut, wrap it once around the needle close to the place where it emerged. Now take the needle to the wrong side, just beside the starting point.

Always take the needle through quickly, so the thread does not have a chance to unwind. For a larger knot, wrap the thread twice around the needle.

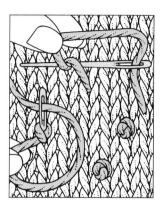

Buttonhole and blanket stitches

These stitches are useful as well as decorative. Worked in the same way, the stitches are called "blanket" when they are spaced apart and "buttonhole" when they are worked close together.

1 Work from left to right. Take the needle to the right, to the desired width of the blanket stitch, then insert it above this point at the desired depth of the stitch (top). Loop the thread around to the right and bring the needle up over it on the lower stitching line. This completes the stitch. Continue working to the right in this way. Secure the last loop as shown (bottom right).

2 You can also work the buttonhole stitch in circles to produce stylized flower shapes.

Lazy daisy stitches being worked.

Couching

Use this stitch to decorate a knitted fabric with yarn that would be difficult or impossible to sew through the fabric. Use a fine sewing thread for the stitching.

1 Lay the main yarn on top of the knitting, leaving a short end free. Bring the stitching thread to the right side, a little beyond the point where the couched thread will be fastened. Stitch over the yarn to be couched and back into the fabric.

2 Make another stitch about ½" (1 cm) further along the stitching line. Continue in this way. After the last stitch, fasten the working thread on the wrong side.

3 Use a blunt-end yarn needle to pull each end of the couched yarn to the wrong side. Using fine thread, sew the yarn ends in place.

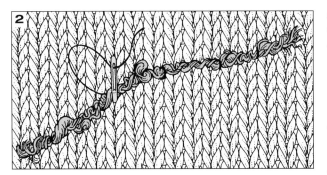

Smocking

As an alternative to knitting in smocking (see page 46), you can embroider the smocking on a knitted fabric. The yarn used for the smocking can be the same yarn as used for the knitting or an embroidery thread. Work the fabric in a K1, P3 rib.

1 Secure the smocking thread at the lower RH corner, to the left of the second rib.

2 Take the thread back over the first rib and up again at the starting point, drawing the two ribs together.

3 Work 2 more backstitches over the ribs, then take the thread under the work and bring it up to the left of the fourth rib.

4 Join the third and fourth ribs in the same way. Work to the end. Work the next row above the first, joining different ribs.

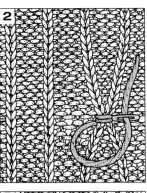

This knitted toy monkey's mouth has been couched in place, giving him a smoother smile than if it had been embroidered.

Decorative cords

Braided and knitted cords are perfect for decorative elements such as drawstrings or ties at a neckline. Experiment using different types of yarn to discover their possibilities.

Braided cord

Cut the strands slightly longer than the required finished length of the cord, making sure that the number of strands is divisible by three. Knot the strands together at one end, and pin the knot to a fixed object, such as the upholstered arm of a chair. Braid the strands. Knot the other end and trim the ends.

Twisted cord

The important thing to remember when making this cord is to twist the strands very tightly, otherwise the finished cord will be flimsy. To estimate how many strands you will need, cut several short strands, twist them together, and then double this twisted length; you can then add or subtract strands as appropriate. Cut the strands for the cord so that they are three times the desired finished length.

1 Knot the strands together at one end, and anchor the knot to a fixed object, such as a doorknob; or ask someone to help you turn from that end.

2 Tie the strands together at the other end, and slip a pencil through the knot.

3 Holding the strands taut, turn the pencil clockwise, continuing to turn until the strands kink up in several places if the tension is relaxed.

4 Bring the two knotted ends together, and give the cord a firm shake; it will twist around itself. Smooth out the coils, and tie a knot a short distance from the folded end. Also knot the two free ends together. Trim both ends and fluff them out.

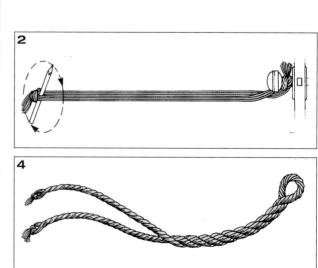

Knitted cord

For this cord you need two double-pointed needles. You only use one strand of yarn, working with the end of yarn still attached to the ball.

1 Cast on 2 (or more) stitches and knit them in the usual way. Without turning the work, slide the stitches to the other end of the needle, bring the yarn firmly from left to right, behind the work, and knit the 2 stitches.

2 Continue in this way until the cord is the required length. Knit the 2 stitches together and fasten off. You can sew the loose yarn ends into the cord, or use them to attach a pom-pom, tassel, or bead to each end.

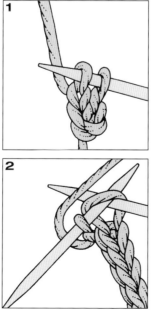

Trimmings

You can decorate many kinds of knitted garment with fringes, tassels, or pom-poms. A simple fringe is the perfect finishing touch for a scarf; a more elaborate knotted one makes an elegant edging on a shawl. Pom-poms make perky trimmings for hats and are a favorite on children's clothes. You can sew a tassel to the ends of knitted cords or attach one to each of the four corners of a knitted (or woven fabric) cushion cover.

Simple fringe

This fringe is essentially a series of tassels. Cut the strands for each tassel about two and a half times the desired finished length.

1 Fold the group of strands in half. With the help of a crochet hook, draw the folded end through the edge from front to back.

2 Bring the strands through the loop, and pull downward gently, bringing the loop up to the edge of the knitting.

This scarf has been finished with a simple fringe.

Knotted fringe

You can create elegant latticelike effects with this technique. The fringe should be at least 4½" (12 cm) deep; it uses fewer strands than a simple fringe.

1 Knot the strands into the edge of the fabric as for a simple fringe, spacing them as desired.

2 When you have attached all the strands, take half the strands from the first group at one edge and half from the next group and tie them together as shown. Join the remaining strands from the second group to half the strands from the third group. Continue to the end.

3 On the next row, separate the strands as in step 2 and tie knots as shown. You can add more rows of knotting if you like. An attractive variation is to join some strands with beads.

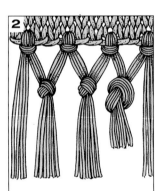

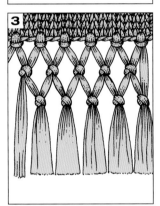

Pom-poms

To make a pom-pom, cut two identical circles from thin cardboard in the diameter of the finished pom-pom. In the center of the circles draw another circle, one quarter the diameter of the outer circle. Cut the center circle out of each larger circle using a pair of sharp scissors.

1 Cut a long length of yarn, thread it into a blunt-end yarn needle, and wrap the yarn around the two circles as shown. Add more yarn until the hole is tightly filled.

2 With sharp scissors cut around the edge of the circles. Pull the cardboard circles apart slightly and tie a length of yarn firmly around the strands in the middle. Cut away the cardboard circles. Fluff out the pom-pom and trim any uneven strands.

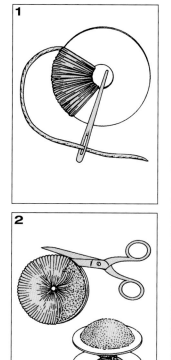

Pom-poms attached to braided cords make a cheerful trim for this hat.

Tassels

From stiff cardboard cut a rectangle the length of the finished tassel.

1 Wind the yarn around the cardboard until the tassel is the desired thickness. Loop a piece of yarn under the strands at one end. Cut through the yarn loops at the other end.

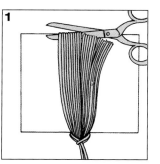

2 Cut a length of yarn, make a loop at one end, and hold the loop alongside the tassel strands. Wind the other end of the yarn around the strands several times. Slip the free end through the loop. Pull on the two ends to fasten them; trim the ends and push them inside the wound yarn.

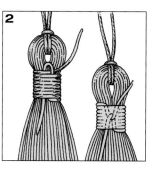

Beads and sequins

For a design that uses many beads or sequins, you should knit them in using one of the following methods. The simpler of the two is the slip-stitch method, while the yarn-around-needle method must be used when working beads into consecutive stitches. Keeping the beads on the right side of the work requires a little more skill here than in the slip-stitch method. You can work them into the knit side or purl side of the work. On the wrong side, work fairly tightly to hold the heads in place.

Threading beads onto yarn

Thread a sewing needle with a double strand of strong thread. Slip the end of the yarn through the loop of thread, and turn back the end. Slide the beads or sequins from the thread onto the yarn, always keeping one bead on the yarn loop to hold it in place.

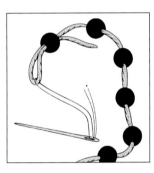

Yarn-around-needle method

1 On a right-side row, insert the needle through the back of the next stitch and push a bead up close to the work.

2 Wrap the yarn around the needle, and push the bead through the stitch to the front. Complete the stitch.

3 On a wrong-side row, insert the needle purlwise through the back of the loop. Push the bead through the loop, and complete the stitch.

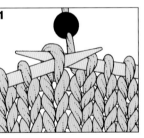

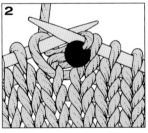

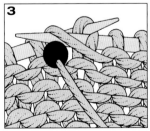

Slip-stitch method

You can used this method wherever the beads or sequins are separated by at least one stitch. It is normally worked on right-side rows, but you can also work from the wrong side. Complete at least two rows of knitting before working in the beads.

1 Knit up to the position for the bead. Bring the yarn forward and slip the next stitch knitwise.

2 Push the bead close to the knitting and knit the next stitch.

3 When working a wrong-side row, with the yarn in back of the work, slip the next stitch purlwise. Push the bead up so that it lies close to the right side and purl the next stitch.

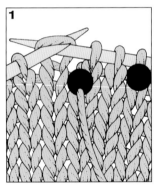

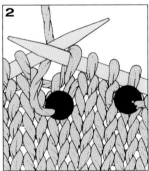

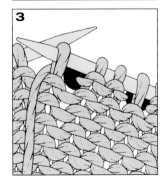

Crochet

Basic crochet techniques are useful for the knitter and are not difficult to learn. You only need one tool, and mistakes are easily corrected; you simply unravel the work back to the mistake, slip the hook into the loop, and continue. You can use crochet to make simple button loops and to finish edges. Crochet is also sometimes used for seams.

Working a chain
(abbreviated ch)

The chain is the basic crochet stitch. A given number of chain stitches are used to begin work and are the equivalent of casting on in knitting.

1 Begin with a slip knot. Leave the hook in the loop, and grasp the base of the knot with the left thumb and forefinger. Slide the hook forward under the tensioned yarn and turn it to catch the yarn as shown.

2 Keeping the yarn tensioned, pull the hook back through the loop to form a new loop.

3 Repeat steps 1 and 2 to complete the chain to the right length.

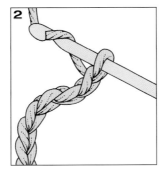

Single crochet
(abbreviated sc)

Work this stitch to provide a neat, firm edge on a completed knitted fabric, perhaps in a different color.

1 Secure the yarn to the RH corner of the work. Insert the hook into the first stitch, front to back, and draw through a loop.

2 Wrap the yarn around the hook and draw this loop through the first loop.

3 Insert the hook into the next stitch and draw through a second loop.

4 Wrap the yarn around the hook and draw it through both loops. One single crochet has been completed. Repeat steps 3 and 4 as required. To turn a corner, work 3 stitches into the corner stitch.

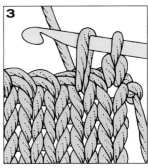
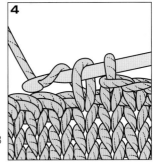

Slip stitch
(abbreviated sl st)

Use this stitch to join two pieces of knitting. Insert the hook through both layers. Draw a loop through the stitch and through the loop on the hook in one movement. Continue in this way along the seam.

Hold the hook and yarn as shown here. The yarn goes around the left little finger, under the second and third finger then over the first finger.

The skills covered here include some that you may need only occasionally, such as inserting a zipper or working a knitted-in hem, as well as skills that will give your knitting a professional touch. These include such refinements as a bias bind-off for slanting shoulder seams, an invisible cast-on edge, how to join knitted edges by grafting rather than sewing them together, and several different kinds of hems and pockets. As you gain experience and confidence as a knitter, you will often find that you can improve on the techniques specified in a commercial pattern. For example, you might wish to knit a patch pocket on picked-up stitches, rather than sew it on. Practice these special techniques and keep the samples for reference later.

Special techniques

Advanced casting on

The two methods of casting on shown here are worth learning. They are often called "invisible" cast-on methods because they employ a separate length of yarn that is later removed. Method 1 is used on a single-rib fabric; when the foundation yarn is removed, the edge that remains appears to consist only of ribbing, although the first four rows are actually produced by a slip-stitch technique. The smooth edge is flexible and attractive, and worth the small amount of extra work involved. In method 2 the edge that remains consists of loose stitches that can either be picked up and knitted (for a lacy edging perhaps) or grafted to another edge for an invisible seam.

Invisible cast on – method 1

Use this method for a single ribbing, worked over an odd number of stitches. Use a contrasting yarn for the initial cast on; it will be removed later.

1 Using the thumb or double cast-on method (easier to remove than the cable method), cast on half the number of stitches required. Round the result up to the next number when the total stitches is an odd number.

2 Join on the main yarn and cut off the contrasting yarn. Work the first 5 rows as follows:
Row 1 (inc row) K1, *YO, K1, rep from * to end. The correct number of stitches should now be on the needle.

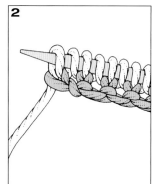

3 Row 2 Wyif sl 1 purlwise, *K1, wyif sl 1 purlwise, rep from * to end.
Row 3 K1, *wyif sl 1 purlwise, K1, rep from * to end.
Row 4 Rep row 2.
Row 5 Rep row 3.

4 Work in K1, P1 rib for the required depth, and then unpick the contrasting yarn.

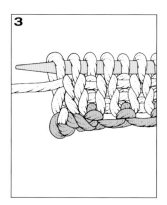

The edge produced by the invisible cast on (method 1) is flexible, attractive, and hard wearing.

Invisible cast on – method 2

Use a contrasting yarn for this method; you will remove it later.

1 Make a slip knot in the main yarn (A) and place it on the needle. Tie the contrasting yarn (B) to the main yarn, and hold the two yarns in the left hand as shown. Take yarn A over the needle from front to back.

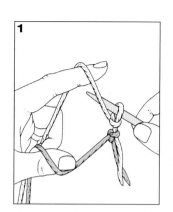

2 Take yarn B over the needle from back to front. The yarns should now be crossed on top of the needle.

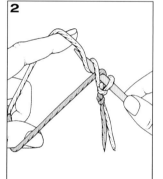

3 Take yarn A over the needle again from front to back, and pull both yarns around the far side of the needle, bringing them below the needle. Recite to yourself, "front to back, back to front, front to back and down." The contrasting yarn should lie in a straight line along the lower edge of the cast-on stitches.

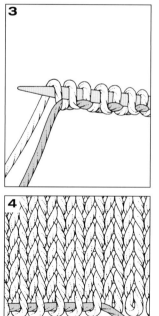

4 When you have cast on the required number of stitches, tie the contrasting yarn to the main yarn at the end, and cut it off. Leave this yarn in place until the knitting is completed, then remove it and pick up the stitches as instructed by the pattern for further knitting or grafting.

Multiple increase

Some patterns will require you to cast on a number of stitches at a side edge in order to work some shaping such as adding a sleeve on a T-shaped garment. Any convenient cast-on method can be used for this; however, if you are using a two-strand method such as the double cast on, you will need to tie an extra strand onto the work.

If you are making an increase at the left-hand edge of the garment (that is, the left edge with the work facing you), cast on the extra stitches immediately after completing a right-side row, so that the first row you work on them will be a wrong-side row. If the increase is to come at the right-hand edge, cast on the stitches after completing a wrong-side row.

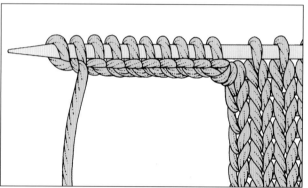

There is no shoulder seam on this Snuggle Cardigan (page 101). The sleeves were knitted as part of the garment, using a multiple increase.

Advanced binding off

Here are four different ways of binding off. The suspended bind off is more flexible than the basic method (see page 16). The bias bind off is a special way of shaping an edge that would otherwise be bound off on alternate rows, producing a stepped effect. The double bind off can be used to join a shoulder seam or any straight edges with the same number of stitches. The invisible bind off is ideal for single ribbing when an inconspicuous finish is desired.

Suspended bind off

You can use this method on ribbing (although the edge is somewhat more conspicuous than a rib bind off) or on garments where elasticity is important.

1 Work the first 2 stitches. *Lift the first stitch over the second, as usual, but leave the lifted stitch on the LH needle.

2 Still leaving the first 2 stitches in place, work the third stitch.

3 Drop the second and third stitches off the LH needle. Two loops are now on the RH needle. Repeat from * until 2 stitches remain; knit these two stitches together.

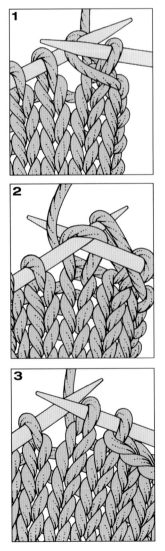

Bias bind off

A pattern instructs you to bind off in stages and gives the exact number of stitches to bind off on each shaping row. The process takes 5 rows, typically. You can easily convert the instructions to make a bias bind off. The left shoulder is shown here.

1 Work up to the last row before the shoulder shaping, ending at the neck edge with a wrong-side row. Work across the stitches up to those to be bound off. Turn, leaving these stitches unworked. Slip the first stitch purlwise.

2 Work across to the end (neck edge). Turn and work across the stitches up to the next group to be bound off. Turn, leaving these stitches unworked. Slip the first stitch purlwise. Work across to the end. Continue until only the last group of stitches remains to be worked. With right side facing, bind off all stitches.

3 The bound-off edge slopes smoothly. To bind off a right shoulder, work as above, reversing the terms "right side" and "wrong side."

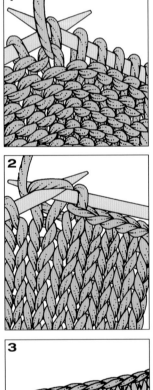

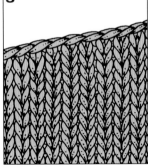

Three-needle bind off

This is a combined bind off and seam, and makes a good finish to a bias bind off. The edges to be joined must have the same number of stitches.

Work the two pieces of knitting up to the last row before binding off; leave the stitches on a spare needle.

Before working the bind off, arrange the two pieces on the needles so that when they are placed together with right sides facing the needles will point to the right.

1 Holding the two pieces together, with right sides facing, insert a third needle knitwise through the first stitch on each piece, and knit the 2 stitches together. Work the next 2 stitches together in the same way.

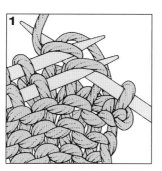

2 Using one of the two needles in the left hand (either will do), lift the first stitch over the second, as for the basic bind off. Repeat both steps until all the stitches have been bound off.

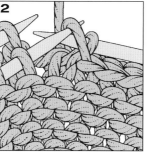

The invisible bind off produces an edge that is ideal for neckline ribbing – or wherever smooth, flexible ribbing is especially important.

Invisible bind off

This ingenious method of binding off a single rib fabric may seem complex at first, but the results are worth the effort. It makes a highly professional finish on a ribbed collar or neckband.

To practice, cast on an odd number of stitches – at least 25 – and work in K1, P1 rib for about 1½" (4 cm), ending with a wrong-side row. Cut the yarn, allowing 3 times the width of the knitting, and thread the end into a tapestry needle. In the illustrations the yarn tail is shown in a contrasting color for clarity. The knit stitches have odd numbers, the purl stitches have even ones.

You work into each stitch twice; the first time in the opposite direction to its construction, the second time in the same direction. Only then do you slip the stitch slipped off the needle.

1 To begin, insert the tapestry needle purlwise into stitch 1, then knitwise into stitch 2. Leave these stitches on the knitting needle. Work knitwise into stitch 1 and slip it off the needle.

2 Work purlwise into stitch 3. Work purlwise into stitch 2 and slip it off the needle.

Take the tapestry needle behind stitch 3 and to the front between stitches 3 and 4. Work knitwise into stitch 4. Repeat steps 2–5, working into stitches 3, 5, 4, and 6 . Continue in this way to the end of the row.

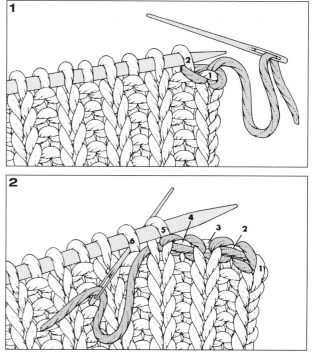

Grafting

Grafting is a method of sewing two knitted edges together stitch by stitch, so that the seam is invisible. The sewing stitches duplicate the structure of the knitting. This technique is often used to join a front and back section at the shoulder, as well as for the toes of socks. The edges need not be straight, as shown; they could be shaped, as shown on page 82. To work the grafting, you can either place the pieces on a flat surface, as shown in these illustrations, or hold them together with wrong sides facing and the needles close together in your hand. Grafting can also be used to join an edge that has been cast on using the invisible method 2 (see page 81).

Grafting garter stitch

Although most often used on stockinette stitch, grafting can be used on other patterns, such as garter stitch.

End one piece on a right-side row, the other on a wrong-side row, so that the lower piece will have a ridge close to the needle and the other piece will have the ridge one row away.

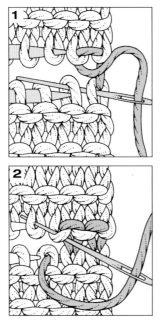

1 Thread a yarn needle with matching yarn, 3 times the width of the knitted edge. Insert the tapestry needle purlwise through the first stitch on the lower edge, purlwise through the first upper stitch and then knitwise through the next upper stitch.

2 *Insert the needle knitwise again through the first lower stitch, then purlwise through the second lower stitch.

3 Insert the needle purlwise through the upper stitch, then knitwise through the next upper stitch. Repeat from * to end.

Grafting stockinette stitch

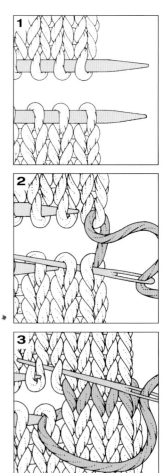

1 End one piece of knitting with a knit row and the other with a purl row, so that when the work is positioned as shown the needles will both point to the right.

2 Thread a yarn needle with matching yarn, 3 times the width of the knitted edge. Insert the needle purlwise through the first stitch on the lower edge, then purlwise through the opposite stitch on the upper edge. Take it knitwise through the first stitch again, then purlwise through the second stitch on the same edge.

3 *Insert the needle knitwise into the stitch on the upper edge where the yarn emerges, then purlwise into the next stitch to the left. Insert it knitwise into the stitch just below, then purlwise into the next stitch to the left. Repeat from * to end.

Hems, facings, and waistbands

Hems are needed wherever a reasonably firm edge that lies flat is required: on the lower and front opening edges of a tailored jacket, for example. A vertical hem is normally called a facing. It is sometimes possible, such as when working a skirt, to work from the top downward, ending with the hem. The hem edge stitches can be bound off, or left on the needle and sewn to the main fabric using the stitch-by-stitch method (see page 86). A knitted waistband is similar to a hem, and is often worked in single ribbing and used on garments for babies or young children, as the extra-snug fit compensates for the lack of a natural waistline. A less bulky alternative to a knitted waistband is a herringbone casing (see page 86).

Sewn-in hem with ridge foldline

This hem is best suited to a garment worked in stockinette stitch. Use a cast-on method with a fairly flat edge.

If you plan to use the stitch-by-stitch sewing method for attaching the hem, use the invisible cast-on method 2 (see page 81). For the hem itself, use needles one or two sizes smaller than those specified for the main fabric. This helps the hem to lie smoothly when turned up.

1 Work in stockinette stitch for the required depth of the hem, ending with a wrong-side row.

2 On the next (right-side) row, purl, rather than knit, to produce a ridge on the fabric. This will serve as the foldline on the hem.

3 Change to larger needles and continue in stockinette stitch for the main part of the garment.

Sewn-in hem with slip-stitch foldline

This hem is more suitable for garments worked in textured stitch patterns or heavyweight yarn.

1 Work the depth of the hem in stockinette stitch, using smaller needles, as for the ridge foldline hem, ending with a wrong-side row.

2 On the next right-side row, work as follows: *K1, wyif sl 1, rep from * to last st, K1.

3 Change to larger needles and work the main part of the garment in pattern.

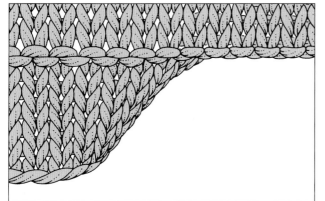

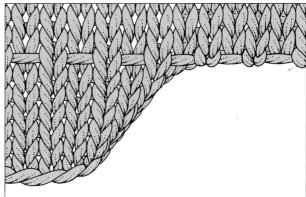

Sewn-in hem with picot foldline

This hem is best worked in a fine yarn.

1 Cast on an odd number of stitches and work in stockinette stitch, using smaller needles, to the desired depth. End with a wrong-side row.

2 On the next (right-side) row, work as follows: *K2tog, YO, rep from * to last st, K1.

3 Change to larger needles, and continue in pattern. When complete, turn up the hem along the line of eyelets to produce the picot effect.

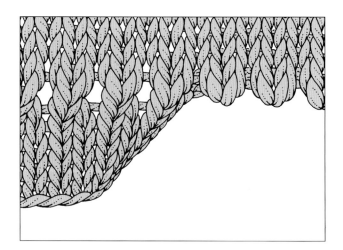

Whipstitch

This stitch is suitable for sewing the hem on a garment worked in a light- or medium-weight yarn. Work through a single purled loop of the main fabric, then through a loop on the hem edge as shown.

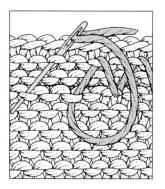

Blind hem stitch

This method is suitable for a heavyweight fabric. You may need to separate the yarn and use only one or two plies for sewing to reduce bulk. First tack the hem in place, about ⅜" (1 cm) below the edge. Turn the garment as shown, with the hem fold away from you. Work the stitches between the hem edge and the main fabric so that the hem edge is free.

Stitch-by-stitch method

You can use this method on an edge that has been cast on using the invisible method 2 or on the edge of a section that has been worked from the top down. In the first case, remove the foundation yarn gradually as you work the hem; in the second, leave the knitting needle in the work, removing it as you stitch.

1 Secure the sewing yarn at the RH edge, and insert the tapestry needle purlwise through the first stitch on the lower edge. Insert it through the corresponding stitch in the main fabric, then knitwise through the first lower stitch. Insert the needle knitwise through the next stitch on the lower edge, then purlwise into the next stitch above.

2 Continue working in this way to the end.

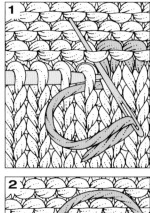

Knitted-in hem

This is an ingenious way of turning up a hem, but you must work it carefully so that it doesn't look bulky. Before knitting the garment itself, work a small sample and adjust the hem needle size and the number of rows if necessary. The needles you use for the hem should be two or three sizes smaller than those used for the main fabric.

1 Cast on the required number of stitches and work the hem allowance as for a sewn-in hem. Work a ridge or slip-stitch foldline (page 85), and continue with the larger needles until the main part of the garment is the same depth as the hem allowance, ending with a wrong-side row. Leave the stitches on the needle.

2 Using a spare needle and a new ball of yarn and working on the right side, pick up and knit stitches along the cast-on edge. Work into the farthest loop of each stitch – the one that is closer to the garment. Fasten off the extra yarn.

3 Turn up the hem along the ridge. Using the main yarn and working on the right side of the garment, knit together 1 stitch from the garment with 1 stitch from the hem all along the row. The picked-up stitches from the hem are now securely knitted into the main fabric.

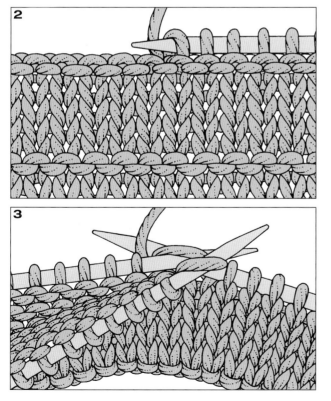

Mitered hem and facing

For a neat finish on the lower edges of a jacket, work a hem and facing with a mitered corner. First calculate, the number of stitches to cast on for the hem by subtracting the number of stitches in 1" (2.5 cm) from the total number of stitches called for in the pattern instructions.

1 Cast on the reduced number of stitches and work in stockinette stitch, increasing 1 stitch at the front edge on every other row until you have the total number of stitches needed on the needle.

2 Work the turning ridge, then continue increasing, working a slip-stitch foldline (above). When the facing is the same depth as the hem, work even to continue.

3 When complete, fold the hem and facing to the wrong side of the garment along their fold lines, and then overcast stitch the diagonal edges neatly together.

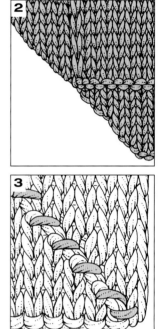

Vertical facing

A vertical facing may be required on the front edge of a jacket, for example, and should always be worked in stockinette stitch. The illustration shows a left front edge; reverse the process for a right front edge.

On a right-side row, work in pattern to the foldline; slip the next stitch purlwise; continue in stockinette stitch to the end of the row. On a wrong-side row, work in stockinette stitch up to and including the slipped stitch; continue in pattern to the end. When the section is complete, turn the facing to the wrong side along the foldline and stitch it in place.

Herringbone casing

1 Cut a piece of elastic that fits the waist smoothly without stretching. Sew the ends of the elastic together to form a ring. Divide the elastic into four equal sections and mark them with pins. Mark the skirt edge into quarters. Pin the elastic to the wrong side of the waist edge, matching the points on the skirt edge.

2 Thread knitting yarn into a tapestry needle and secure to the fabric with two backstitches, just below the elastic. Take the needle up over the elastic and to the right, and insert it through the edge of the knitting from right to left. Take it down to the right and insert it again from the left. Continue around the waistband; secure firmly.

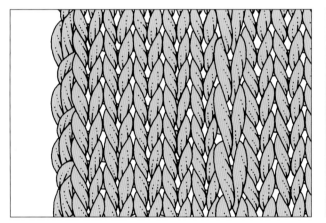

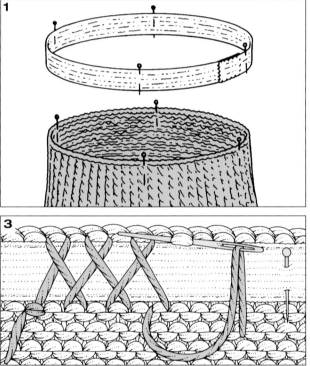

Knitted waistband

1 Work a ridge foldline as shown on page 85, then knit the waistband in K1, P1 rib until you have reached the required depth.

2 Sew the waistband in place, leaving about 2" (5 cm) unstitched.

3 Insert elastic through the casing, and pin the ends together with a safety pin. Adjust the fit as necessary before sewing the ends together firmly. Complete the stitching on the casing edge to finish.

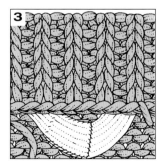

Pockets

The three most popular styles of pocket are the patch pocket, the horizontal inside pocket and the vertical inside pocket. There are various methods of working them; you can often substitute a method you prefer for the one called for in a pattern. Patch pockets are usually most successful in a textured stitch pattern, which provides contrast. A stockinette-stitch patch pocket can have a homemade look if it is not sewn on carefully. If a stockinette-stitch pocket is required, an attractive way of attaching it is with duplicate stitching. Alternately, work a modified patch pocket on stitches picked up from the main fabric. Working a garter stitch selvage along the two sides will provide a neat finish. You can attach a patch pocket leaving the outer side edge open (unstitched) instead of the top edge.

Duplicate stitching a patch pocket

1 Work the patch to the desired size and bind off. Block or press it as appropriate, and weave in the ends. Pin the pocket to the garment. Secure the yarn (shown here in a contrasting color for clarity) to the lower RH corner on the wrong side of the main fabric, and bring it up in the center of the first stitch in from the edge.

2 Duplicate stitch (see page 70) over all the stitches across the lower edge of the pocket.

3 Continue up the LH side of the pocket as shown. Sew the RH edge of the pocket in the same way.

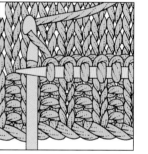

Patch pocket on picked-up stitches

This style of pocket is also worked after the main section has been completed.

1 Secure the yarn to the wrong side of the work at the position of the lower RH corner of the pocket. Using a crochet hook, pick up the required number of stitches for the pocket and place them on the knitting needle.

2 Beginning with a purl row, work in stockinette stitch to the required depth for the pocket. Bind off evenly.

3 Sew the side edges of the pocket in place, either with duplicate stitch or the overcast stitch.

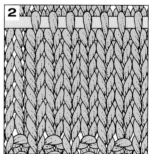

Overcasting a patch pocket

1 Lay the pocket on the main section, and insert a pin diagonally at each corner, pinning through the background fabric only. Remove the pocket, and check that the pins are aligned on the same vertical and horizontal rows.

2 Insert two fine double-pointed needles in the fabric between the pins, picking up every other stitch.

3 Place the pocket between the needles, and sew it to the picked-up stitches, working into the alternating stitches along the pocket edge. When both sides have been sewn, sew the lower edge in place, again working through every other stitch.

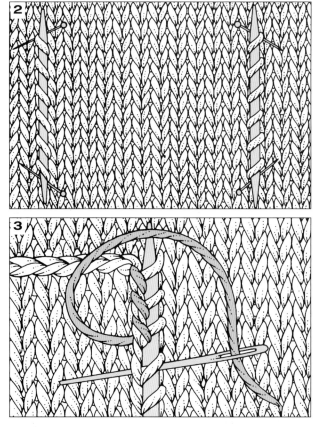

Horizontal inside pocket

A pattern will often instruct you to place a horizontal pocket by leaving the stitches for the border on a spare needle, joining in the pocket lining and then picking up the opening stitches and working the border. The following method incorporates the border stitches in the fabric, producing a slightly neater finish.

1 First work the pocket lining, casting on 2 more stitches than are allowed for the opening. Work the lining to the required depth, ending with a knit row and decreasing 1 stitch at each end of the previous purl row. Leave the stitches on a spare needle.

2 Work the main fabric up to the position for the pocket border. Continue knitting, working the border in the chosen pattern. When the border is the required depth, bind off these stitches on a right-side row; work to the end of row.

3 On the next row, purl across to the beginning of the pocket opening, then purl across the stitches of the pocket lining and continue to the end of the row.

4 When the section is complete, overcast the pocket lining edges in place on the wrong side.

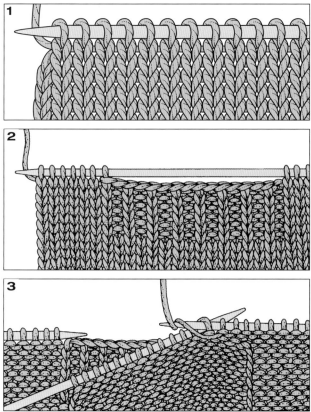

Vertical pockets with borders included

You work the opening for a vertical pocket in two stages, first one side and then the other. When the second side is as deep as the first, you rejoin the two sides. You can then incorporate a pocket lining in the outer side section of the fabric. You can either knit the border of a vertical pocket along with the top part of the pocket or work it later on picked-up stitches. The illustrations show a pocket in the right front of a garment. For the left front, reverse the instructions.

1 Work a few rows of stockinette stitch for the lower part of the pocket lining. End with a right-side row, and place the stitches on a spare needle.

2 Work the garment front up to the level for the pocket opening, ending with a wrong-side row. On the next row, work across to the pocket inner edge of the border, then work in the border pattern (P1, K1 rib shown here) across the specified number of stitches. Slip the remaining stitches for the garment onto a spare needle.

3 Continue working on the top section of the pocket until it is the required depth, ending with a right-side row. Slip these stitches on to a spare needle; do not break off the yarn. Now pick up the pocket lining; place it alongside the garment side section, join on new yarn if necessary, and knit to the end of the row.

4 Continue working across the garment and pocket lining until this piece is one row shorter than the top section, ending with a wrong-side row. On the next row, bind off the pocket lining stitches. Rejoin the two sections of the main fabric; knit to the end of the row. Whipstitch the pocket lining to the main fabric.

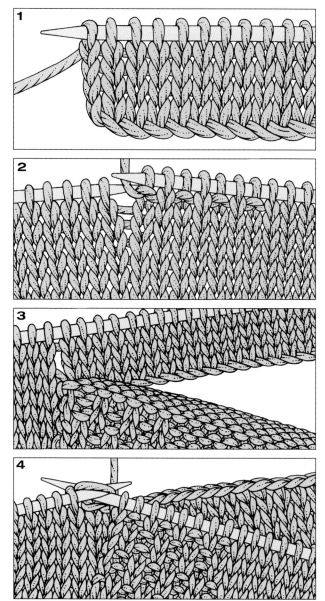

Pocket with border added

Work this pocket as for the one with a knitted border, but do not work the border stitches. (The division should be placed slightly closer to the center front.) When the section is completed, pick up stitches along the edge of the top section of the pocket and work in the chosen pattern (P1, K1 rib shown here). Sew the edges to the main fabric.

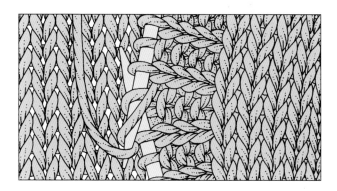

Closures

Closures can be problematic in a knitted garment because the fabric is soft and stretchy and is inclined to pull away from a zipper or buttons. When inserting a zipper, it is important to provide a firm edge for the zipper opening. When knitting with a heavyweight yarn, this is best done by working a selvage; for lightweight yarn, use crochet.

Inserting a zipper – selvage opening

When working the garment, add 2 stitches to the opening edges, and work a double garter stitch selvage (see page 27). Block or press the completed sections.

1 Place the adjacent sections right side up, and tack them together using an overcast stitch, a blunt-end yarn needle, and sewing thread.

2 Turn the work wrong side up. Open the zipper and place it over the opening with the teeth exactly centered. Using an ordinary sewing needle, tack one side of the zipper tape to the knitting. Close the zipper and tack the other side.

3 Working from the right side and using strong sewing thread such as buttonhole twist, sew the zipper in place with a backstitch. Start at the top and work down one side and up the other.

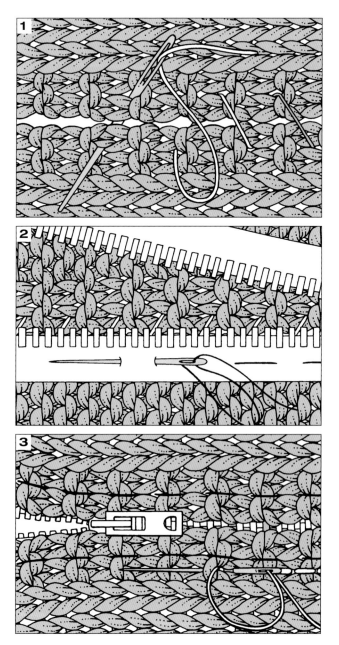

Crocheted zipper opening

1 Before sewing in the zipper, work a row of single crochet (see page 77) along the opening edges.

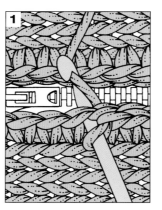

2 Tack and stitch the zipper in place as described for a selvage opening (see opposite), working the backstitch along the outer edge of the crochet.

3 Open the zipper and work crochet slip stitches (see page 77) into the single crochet stitches.

Ribbon-faced buttonhole band

To prevent the button and buttonhole bands of a cardigan from sagging, sew a length of ribbon (grosgrain is the usual choice, but any firm ribbon will do) to the underside of the bands.

1 Cut the ribbon about 1¼" (3 cm), longer than the band. Turn under one end and tack it to the knitting; trim the other end if necessary, and turn it under. Slip stitch the ribbon in place as shown.

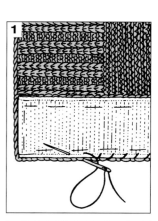

2 To finish, turn the buttonhole band right side up and cut a slit in the ribbon under each buttonhole, taking care not to cut into the knitting. Using yarn or matching pearl cotton and a chenille needle (a large-eyed sharp-pointed embroidery needle), work the buttonhole stitch around the buttonholes.

This zipper has been worked into the firm bound-off edge of the Checked Pillow (page 152) so there is no need for selvage.

There is no greater joy than receiving a hand-knitted gift for a new baby. Moms and dads delight in cute knitted hats and booties, and really appreciate the personal touch they contribute to the occasion; hand-knitted baby items are often treasured for years to come. You can choose from a handful of lovely projects: a blanket for a newborn, tiny baby slippers, a snuggle cardigan, and a cozy hat and mittens. All of the projects are either easy or intermediate skill level and can be adapted for boys or girls simply by changing the colorways.

Beautiful for babies

Baby blanket

This stripy blanket is fun to knit – and relatively quick to make, as finishing is minimal. With its fresh color scheme, it will give a touch of class to any nursery.

Skill level
Intermediate

Techniques
- Yarn over increase (page 30)
- Knitting two stitches together (page 31)
- Slipped stitch decrease (page 32)
- Intarsia (pages 62–63)
- Weaving in ends (page 37)

Tools
1 pair of US 8 (5 mm) knitting needles
Basic equipment for finishing (see page 35)

Materials
Rowan All Seasons Cotton
3 balls of 50 g (1¾ oz) yarn in Bleached, 182 **(A)**

3 balls in Lime Leaf, 217 **(B)**

3 balls in Ravish, 199 **(C)**

Gauge
17 sts and 24 rows to 4" (10 cm) measured over St st on US 8 (5 mm) needles. Change needle size if necessary to obtain correct gauge.

Abbreviations
See page 6.

Note
When changing color always twist the yarns on the WS of your work, as explained for intarsia (see pages 62–63), to avoid leaving a hole.

Measurements
Finished size:
34½" × 26¾"
(88 cm × 68 cm)

Blanket

Using yarn A, cast on 25 sts, using B cast on 25 sts, using C cast on 25 sts, using A cast on 25 sts, using B cast on 25 sts, using C cast on 25 sts. 150 sts.

Keeping each color correct and twisting yarns at back of work, cont as follows:

Row 1: Knit.

Row 2: Purl.

Now work in diamond patt as follows:

Row 1: *K11, YO, sl 1, K2tog, psso, YO, K11, rep from * to end.

Row 2 and all even-numbered rows: Purl.

Row 3: *K10, K2tog, YO, K1, YO, sl 1, K1, psso, K10, rep from * to end.

Row 5: *K9, K2tog, YO, K3, YO, sl 1, psso, K9, rep from * to end.

Row 7: *K8, K2tog, YO, K5, YO, sl 1, K1, psso, K8, rep from * to end.

Row 9: *K7, K2tog, YO, K7, YO, sl 1, K1, psso, K7, rep from * to end.

Row 11: *K6, K2tog, YO, K9, YO, sl 1, K1, psso, K6, rep from * to end.

Row 13: *K5, K2tog, YO, K11, YO, sl 1, K1, psso, K5, rep from * to end.

Row 15: *K4, K2tog, YO, K13, YO, sl 1, K1, psso, K4, rep from * to end.

Row 17: *K3, K2tog, YO, K15, YO, sl 1, K1, psso, K3, rep from * to end.

Row 19: *K2, K2tog, YO, K17, YO, sl 1, K1, psso, K2, rep from * to end.

Row 21: *K1, K2tog, YO, K19, YO, sl 1, K1, psso, K1, rep from * to end.

Row 23: *K2, YO, sl 1, K1, psso, K17, K2tog, YO, K2, rep from * to end.

Row 25: *K3, YO, sl 1, K1, psso, K15, K2tog, YO, K3, rep from * to end.

Row 27: *K4, YO, sl 1, K1, psso, K13, K2tog, YO, K4, rep from * to end.

Row 29: *K5, YO, sl 1, K1, psso, K11, K2tog, YO, K5, rep from * to end.

Row 31: *K6, YO, sl 1, K1, psso, K9, K2tog, YO, K6, rep from * to end.

Row 33: *K7, YO, sl 1, K1, psso, K7, K2tog, YO, K7, rep from * to end.

Row 35: *K8, YO, sl 1, K1, psso, K5, K2tog, YO, K8, rep from * to end.

Row 37: *K9, YO, sl 1, K1, psso, K3, K2tog, YO, K9, rep from * to end

Row 39: *K10, YO, sl 1, K1, psso, K1, K2tog, YO, K10, rep from * to end.

Row 40: Purl.

These 40 rows form diamond patt. Cont in diamond patt, rep rows 1–40 three more times, then work rows 1 and 2 again. Bind off in each color.

Next Row: Knit.

Next Row: Purl.

To finish

Weave in loose ends. Press carefully, following instructions on yarn label and using a pressing cloth.

Baby slippers

These adorable little slippers make a charming gift for a new baby and will be treasured in years to come as a reminder of tiny infant feet.

Skill level
Intermediate

Techniques
- Garter stitch (page 19)
- Bar increase (page 28)
- Knitting or purling two stitches together (page 31)
- Multiple increase (page 81)
- Weaving in ends (page 37)
- Seams (page 36)

Tools
1 pair of US 8 (4 mm) knitting needles
Basic equipment for finishing (see page 35)

Materials
Rowan Kid Classic
1 ball of 50 g (1¾ oz) yarn in Glacier, 822
or
Feather, 828

24" (60 cm) of coordinating organza ribbon

Gauge
22 sts and 40 rows to 4" (10 cm) measured over garter st using US 6 needles. Change needle size if necessary to obtain correct gauge.

Abbreviations
See page 6.

Measurements

Size			
To fit:	0–3 months	3–6 months	6–9 months
Actual measurements			
Length of foot:	3½" (9 cm)	4" (10 cm)	4½" (11 cm)

Slippers

Cast on 14 (14, 16) sts.

Working in garter st throughout, as follows:

Inc 1 st at each end of next row and EOR 2 (3, 3) times. 20 (22, 24) sts.

Work 3 (1, 3) rows even.

Dec 1 st at each end of next row and EOR 2 (3, 3) times, ending with WS facing for next row. 14 (14, 16) sts. This completes sole section.

Shape heel:

Cast on 4 (5, 6) sts at beg of next row. 18 (19, 22) sts.

Inc 1 st at beg of next row and EOR 2 (3, 3) times, ending with WS facing for next row. 21 (23, 26) sts.

Shape foot opening:

Bind off 12 (13, 15) sts at beg of next row (for foot opening). 9 (10, 11) sts.

Work 9 (11, 15) rows, ending with WS facing for next row.

Shape second side of heel:

Cast on 12 (13, 15) sts at beg of next row (for other side of foot opening). 21 (23, 26) sts.

Dec 1 st at beg of next row and EOR 2 (3, 3) times. Bind off rem 18 (19, 22) sts.

To finish

Do *not* press.

Weave in ends. Sew together row-end edges of heel sections. Easing in fullness, sew upper section to sole along heel, toe, and side edges. Cut ribbon into 4 equal lengths and sew to sides of foot opening. Tie ends in a bow on top of foot.

Snuggle cardigan

A versatile extra layer that will look and feel great over a simple one-piece garment or a party dress

Skill level
Intermediate

Techniques
- Bar increase (page 28)
- Knitting or purling two stitches together (page 31)
- Multiple increase (page 81)
- Pressing (page 35)
- Seams (page 36)
- Picking up stitches (page 33)
- Eyelet buttonhole (page 34)
- Weaving in ends (page 37)

Tools
1 pair of US 3 (3.25 mm) knitting needles
1 pair of US 6 (4 mm) knitting needles

2 stitch markers
1 stitch holder
Basic equipment for finishing (see page 35)

Materials
 Rowan Wool Cotton
3 (3, 4, 5) balls of 50 g (1¾ oz) in Clear, 941 **(A)**

1 ball in Antique, 900 **(B)**

Alternative colors
Variation 1
Antique, 900 **(A)**

 Bilberry Fool, 959 **(B)**

Variation 2
Citron, 901 **(A)**

Elf, 946 **(B)**

5 buttons

Gauge
23 sts and 32 rows to 4" (10 cm) measured over pattern using US 6 needles. Change needle size if necessary to obtain correct gauge.

Abbreviations
See page 6.

Measurements

Size	1	2	3	4
To fit:	0–3 months	3–6 months	6–12 months	12–18 months
Chest:	16" (41 cm)	18" (46 cm)	20" (51 cm)	22" (56 cm)
Actual measurements				
Chest:	18" (46 cm)	20" (51 cm)	22½" (57 cm)	24½" (62 cm)
Length:	8¼" (21 cm)	9¾" (25 cm)	11½" (29 cm)	13" (33 cm)
Sleeve seam:	4¾" (12 cm)	6" (15 cm)	7½" (19 cm)	8½" (22 cm)

Body

The body is worked in one piece, starting at back cast-on edge.

Using smaller needles and yarn B, cast on 53 (59, 65, 71) sts.

Rows 1–3: Using B, knit.

Join in A.

Rows 4 and 5: Using A, knit.

Rows 6 and 7: Using B, knit.

Break off B and cont using A only.

Change to larger needles.

Work in patt as follows:

Row 1 (RS): Knit.

Row 2: Purl.

Row 3: K1, *P1, K1, rep from * to end.

Row 4: Purl.

These 4 rows form patt.

Cont in patt until Back measures 2¼ (3½, 4¾, 6)" [6 (9, 12, 15) cm], ending with RS facing for next row.

Shape for sleeves:

Inc 1 st at each end of next row and every 4 rows twice, then on EOR twice, and then on next 3 rows, taking inc sts into patt and ending with RS facing for next row. 69 (75, 81, 87) sts.

Cast on 15 (22, 31, 39) sts at beg of next 2 rows. 99 (119, 143, 165) sts.

Work even until work measures 4 (4¼, 4¾, 5)" [10 (11, 12, 13) cm] from sleeve cast-on sts, ending with RS facing for next row.

Divide for fronts:

Place a marker at both ends of last row to denote shoulder "seam."

Next row (RS): Work 39 (48, 59, 69) sts in patt and slip these sts on to a holder for right front. Bind off next 21 (23, 25, 27) sts (for back neck), work in patt to end. Work on this last set of 39 (48, 59, 69) sts only for left front.

Work 3 rows, ending with RS facing for next row.

Inc 1 st at neck edge of next row and then on EOR twice, then on next 3 rows, taking inc sts into patt and ending with RS facing for next row. 45 (54, 65, 75) sts.

Cast on 3 (4, 5, 6) sts at beg of next row. 48 (58, 70, 81) sts.

Work even 4 (4¼, 4¾, 5)" [10 (11, 12, 13) cm] from marker, ending with WS facing for next row.

Shape for sleeve:

Keeping in patt, bind off 15 (22, 31, 39) sts at beg of next row. 33 (36, 39, 42) sts.

Work 1 row even.

Dec 1 st at sleeve edge on next 4 rows, then on EOR twice, then on every 4th row twice. 25 (28, 31, 34) sts.

Work even until work measures 1½ (2¾, 4, 5)" [4 (7, 10, 13) cm] from sleeve bound-off sts, ending with RS facing for next row.

Change to smaller needles.

Join in B.

Using B, knit 2 rows.

Using A, knit 2 rows.

Using B, knit 3 rows, ending with WS facing for next row.

Bind off knitwise on WS.

Place sts holder onto needle, rejoin yarn with WS facing and patt to end. Complete right front to match left front, reversing shaping.

To finish

Press carefully following instructions on yarn label.

Neckband:

With RS facing, using smaller needles and B, and starting and ending at top of front opening edges, PU 15 (16, 17, 18) sts up right side of front neck, 21 (23, 25, 27) sts from back neck bound-off edge, then 15 (16, 17, 18) sts down left side of front neck. 51 (55, 59, 63) sts.

**Row 1 (WS): Using B, knit.

Join in A.

Rows 2 and 3: Using A, knit.

Rows 4–6: Using B, knit.

Using B, bind off knitwise on WS. **

Button band:

With RS facing, using smaller needles and B, PU 43 (51, 63, 71) sts evenly along one front opening edge (left front for a girl, right front for a boy), between top of neckband and front bound-off edge.

Work as for neckband from ** to **.

Buttonhole band:

Work as for button band, picking up sts along other front opening edge and working 5 buttonholes in row 2 as follows:

Row 2 (RS): K2, *K2tog, YO (to make a buttonhole), K7 (9, 12, 14), rep from * 3 more times, K2tog, YO (to make 5th buttonhole), K3.

Cuffs (make 2 alike):

With RS facing, using smaller needles and B, PU 39 (43, 47, 51) sts evenly along row-end edge of sleeve section.

Work as given for neckband from ** to **.

Sew side and sleeve seams. Weave in loose ends. Sew on buttons.

Baby's hat and mittens

Perfect for chilly days outside, this hat and mitten set will feel wonderfully soft on a baby's delicate skin.

Skill level
Easy

Techniques
- Knitting two stitches together (page 31)
- Horizontal stripes (page 60)
- Weaving in ends (page 37)
- Pressing (page 35)
- Seams (page 36)

Tools
1 pair of US 2 (2.75 mm) knitting needles
1 pair of US 3 (3.25 mm) knitting needles
Basic equipment for finishing (see page 35)

Materials
Rowan 4-ply Soft
1 ball of 50 g (1¾ oz) yarn in Whisper, 395 **(A)**

1 ball in Nippy, 376 **(B)**

Alternative colors
Variation 1
Fairy, 370 **(A)**

Nippy, 376 **(B)**

Variation 2
Irish Cream, 386 **(A)**

Nippy, 376 **(B)**

Gauge
28 sts and 36 rows to 4" (10 cm) measured over pattern using US 3 needles. Change needle size if necessary to obtain correct gauge.

Abbreviations
See page 6.

Measurements – Hat

Size	1	2	3	4
To fit:	0–3 months	3–6 months	6–12 months	12–18 months
Circumference:	13¾" (35 cm)	14½" (37 cm)	15¼" (39 cm)	16" (41 cm)

Measurements – Mittens

Size	1	2	3
Finished size:	5" × 3¼" (13 × 8.5 cm)	6¼" × 3¾" (16 × 9.5 cm)	7½" × 4" (19 × 10.5 cm)

Hat

Using larger needles and yarn A, cast on 97 (103, 109, 115) sts.

Row 1 (RS): K1, *P1, K1, rep from * to end.

Row 2: P1, *K1, P1, rep from * to end.

These 2 rows form rib patt.

Join in B.

Using B, work in rib for 2 rows.

Using A, work in rib for 2 rows.

Rep last 4 rows until hat measures 3" (8 cm), ending after 2 rows using B.

Break off B and cont using A only.

Now work in patt as follows:

Row 1 (RS): Knit.

Row 2 and all even-numbered rows: Purl.

Row 3: K3, P1, *K5, P1, rep from * to last 3 sts, K3.

Row 5: Knit.

Row 7: P1, *K5, P1, rep from * to end.

Row 8: Purl.

These 8 rows form patt.

Cont in patt until hat measures 6 (6¼, 6½, 7)" [15 (16, 17, 18) cm], ending with RS facing for next row.

Shape crown:

Row 1 (RS): *K4, K2tog, rep from * to last st, K1. 81 (86, 91, 96) sts.

Row 2: Purl.

Row 3: Knit.

Row 4: Purl.

Row 5: *K3, K2tog, rep from * to last st, K1. 65 (69, 73, 77) sts.

Rows 6–8: Work as for rows 2–4.

Row 9: *K2, K2tog, rep from * to last st, K1. 49 (52, 55, 58) sts.

Row 10: Purl.

Row 11: *K1, K2tog, rep from * to last st, K1. 33 (35, 37, 39) sts.

Row 12: Purl.

Row 13: *K2tog, rep from * to last st, K1. 17 (18, 19, 20) sts.

Row 14: P1 (0, 1, 0), (P2tog) 8 (9, 9, 10) times.

Break yarn and thread it through rem 9 (9, 10, 10) sts. Pull tight and fasten off securely.

To finish hat

Press carefully, following instructions on yarn label.

Weave in loose ends.

Sew back seam, reversing seam for first 2¼" (6 cm) for brim. Fold 1½" (4 cm) to outside.

Mittens (make 4)

Using smaller needles and yarn B, cast on 19 (23, 27) sts.

Row 1: K1, *P1, K1, rep from * to end.

Row 2: P1, *K1, P1, rep from * to end.

These 2 rows form rib.

Join in A.

Using A, work in rib for 2 rows.

Using B, work in rib for 2 rows.

Rep last 4 rows once more.

Change to larger needles and A.

Work in patt as follows:

Row 1 (RS): Knit.

Row 2 and all even-numbered rows: Purl.

Row 3: K3 (5, 7), P1, K5, P1, K5, P1, K3 (5, 7).

Row 5: Knit.

Row 7: K0 (2, 4), P1, K5, P1, K5, P1, K5, P1, K0 (2, 4).

Row 8: Purl.

These 8 rows form patt. Cont in patt until mitten measures 2¾ (3, 3½)" [7 (8, 9) cm].

Keeping in patt, dec 1 st at each end of next 6 rows. Bind off rem 7 (11, 15) sts.

To finish mittens

Weave in loose ends. Block the pieces. Place 2 mitten pieces together with right sides facing and sew together along both side edges and across top edges using backstitch or an edge-to-edge seam. Turn right side out.

Children always look adorable in hand-knit clothes and here are four great projects for toddlers and young children from one to six years old. Knit a rugged hoodie in bold stripes for an adventurous boy's outdoor exploits, or opt for the cozy, cutesy heart-patterned sweater for a girl who loves pink. For keeping snug outside, no trend-setting toddler should be without the fabulous tassel hat, and if you feel ready for a challenge, the scarf and mittens combo is worth the extra effort.

Cute for kids

Rugged hoodie

Perfect for chilly days, this cotton cover-up will make a great addition to any discerning young child's wardrobe!

Skill level
Intermediate

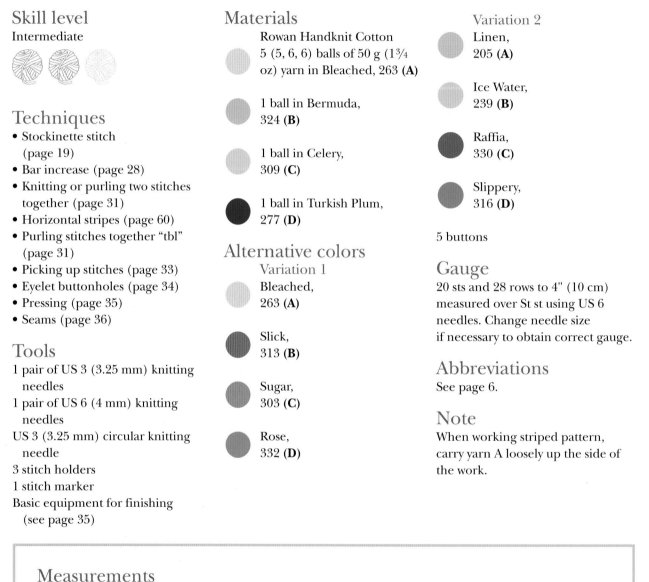

Techniques
- Stockinette stitch (page 19)
- Bar increase (page 28)
- Knitting or purling two stitches together (page 31)
- Horizontal stripes (page 60)
- Purling stitches together "tbl" (page 31)
- Picking up stitches (page 33)
- Eyelet buttonholes (page 34)
- Pressing (page 35)
- Seams (page 36)

Tools
1 pair of US 3 (3.25 mm) knitting needles
1 pair of US 6 (4 mm) knitting needles
US 3 (3.25 mm) circular knitting needle
3 stitch holders
1 stitch marker
Basic equipment for finishing (see page 35)

Materials
Rowan Handknit Cotton
5 (5, 6, 6) balls of 50 g (1¾ oz) yarn in Bleached, 263 (**A**)

1 ball in Bermuda, 324 (**B**)

1 ball in Celery, 309 (**C**)

1 ball in Turkish Plum, 277 (**D**)

Alternative colors
Variation 1
Bleached, 263 (**A**)

Slick, 313 (**B**)

Sugar, 303 (**C**)

Rose, 332 (**D**)

Variation 2
Linen, 205 (**A**)

Ice Water, 239 (**B**)

Raffia, 330 (**C**)

Slippery, 316 (**D**)

5 buttons

Gauge
20 sts and 28 rows to 4" (10 cm) measured over St st using US 6 needles. Change needle size if necessary to obtain correct gauge.

Abbreviations
See page 6.

Note
When working striped pattern, carry yarn A loosely up the side of the work.

Measurements

Size	1	2	3	4
To fit:	1–2 years	2–3 years	3–4 years	4–5 years
Chest:	18" (46 cm)	20" (51 cm)	22" (56 cm)	24" (61 cm)
Actual measurements				
Chest:	22¾" (58 cm)	25¼" (64 cm)	27½" (70 cm)	30" (76 cm)
Length:	10½" (27 cm)	12¼" (31 cm)	13¾" (35 cm)	15¾" (40 cm)
Sleeve seam:	6¼" (16 cm)	7¾" (20 cm)	10¼" (26 cm)	11¾" (30 cm)

Back

Using smaller pair of needles and yarn A, cast on
58 (62, 70, 74) sts.
Row 1 (RS): K2, *P2, K2, rep from * to end.
Row 2: P2, *K2, P2, rep from * to end.
These 2 rows form rib patt.
Work in rib patt for 6 more rows, inc 0 (1, 0, 1) sts at
each end of last row and ending with RS facing for next
row. 58 (64, 70, 76) sts.
Change to larger needles.
Starting with a knit row and joining in colors as
required, work in striped St st patt as follows:
Rows 1 and 2: Using A.
Rows 3–6: Using B.
Rows 7 and 8: Using A.
Rows 9–12: Using C.
Rows 13 and 14: Using A.
Rows 15–18: Using D.
These 18 rows form striped patt.
Cont in patt until back measures 5½ (6½, 7¾, 9½)"
[14 (17, 20, 24) cm], ending with RS facing for next
row.
Shape armholes:
Cont in stripe patt, bind off 3 sts at beg of next 2 rows.
52 (58, 64, 70) sts.
Dec 1 st at each end of next row and then EOR 3 times.
44 (50, 56, 62) sts.
Work even until armhole measures approx 5 (5½, 6,
6¼, 7)" [13 (14, 15, 16) cm], ending after 2 rows using
A and with RS facing for next row.
Break off B, C, and D and cont using A only.
Shape shoulders:
Bind off 4 (5, 5, 6) sts at beg of next 4 rows, and
4 (4, 6, 6) sts at beg of the foll 2 rows.
Break yarn and leave rem 20 (22, 24, 26) sts on a
holder.

Left front

Using smaller needles and A, cast on 27 (31, 31, 35) sts.
Row 1 (RS): K2, *P2, K2, rep from * to last st, K1.
Row 2: K1, P2, *K2, P2, rep from * to end.
These 2 rows form rib patt.
Work in rib patt for 6 more rows, dec (dec, inc, inc)
0 (1, 2, 1) sts evenly across last row and ending with
RS facing for next row. 27 (30, 33, 36) sts.
Change to larger needles.
Starting with a knit row and joining in colors as
required, work in striped patt as given for back until left
front matches back to start of armhole shaping, ending
with RS facing for next row.

Shape armhole:
Cont in stripe patt, bind off 3 sts at beg of next row.
24 (27, 30, 33) sts.
Work 1 row even.
Dec 1 st at armhole edge of next row and then EOR
3 times. 20 (23, 26, 29) sts.
Work straight until left front matches back to start of
shoulder shaping, ending with RS facing for next row.
Break off B, C, and D and C and cont using A only.
Shape shoulder:
Bind off 4 (5, 5, 6) sts at beg of next 2 RS rows, then
4 (4, 6, 6) sts at beg of foll RS row.
Work 1 row even, ending with RS facing for next row.
Break yarn and leave rem 8 (9, 10, 11) sts on a holder.

Right front

Using smaller pair of needles and A, cast on 27 (31, 31,
35) sts.
Row 1 (RS): K3, *P2, K2, rep from * to end.
Row 2: P2, *K2, P2, rep from * to last st, K1.
These 2 rows form rib patt.
Work in rib for 6 more rows, dec (dec, inc, inc) 0 (1, 2,
1) sts evenly across last row and ending with RS facing
for next row. 27 (30, 33, 36) sts.
Change to larger needles.
Starting with a knit row and joining in colors as
required, work in striped patt as given for back until
right front matches back to start of armhole shaping,
ending with WS facing for next row.
Shape armhole:
Cont in stripe patt, bind off 3 sts at beg of next row.
24 (27, 30, 33) sts.
Dec 1 st at armhole edge of next 4 WS rows. 20 (23, 26,
29) sts.
Work even until right front matches back to start of
shoulder shaping, ending with RS facing for next row.
Break off B, C, and D and cont using A only.
Work 1 row even, ending with WS facing for next row.
Shape shoulder:
Bind off 4 (5, 5, 6) sts at beg of next 2 WS rows, and
then 4 (4, 6, 6) sts at beg of foll WS row, ending with RS
facing for next row.
Break yarn and leave rem 8 (9, 10, 11) sts on a holder.

Sleeves

Using smaller needles and A, cast on 26 (30, 30, 32) sts. Work in rib as given for back for 8 rows, inc 1 (0, 1, 0) st at each end of last row and ending with RS facing for next row. 28 (30, 32, 34) sts.

Change to larger needles.

Joining in colors as required, starting with a knit row and stripe row 1, work in striped patt as given for back, shaping sides by inc 1 st at each end of 3rd (3rd, 3rd, 5th) row and then EOR 7 (5, 0, 0) times, and then on every 4th row 0 (1, 3, 3) times. 44 (44, 40, 42) sts.

Work 1 (1, 3, 1) rows, ending after 4 rows using D and with RS facing for next row.

Break off B, C, and D and cont using A only.

Inc 1 st at each end of next (3rd, next, 3rd) row and then every 4th row until there are 48 (56, 60, 60) sts.

First and fourth sizes only:
Inc 1 st at each end of every 4th (6th) row until there are 52 (64) sts.

All sizes:
Work even until sleeve measures 6¼ (7¾, 10¼, 11¾)" [16 (20, 26, 30) cm], ending with RS facing for next row.

Shape top:
Bind off 3 sts at beg of next 2 rows. 46 (50, 54, 58) sts.
Dec 1 st at each end of next row and then on EOR twice, then on the next row once, ending with RS facing for next row.
Bind off rem 38 (42, 46, 50) sts.

To finish

Press carefully following instructions on yarn label.
Sew both shoulder seams.

Hood:
With RS facing, using larger needles and A, work across 8 (9, 10, 11) sts left on right front holder as follows, K4, (M1, K1) 4 (5, 6, 7) times, work across 20 (22, 24, 26) sts from back holder as follows, K1, (M1, K1) 19 (21, 23, 25) times, then work across 8 (9, 10, 11) sts from left front holder as follows: (K1, M1) 4 (5, 6, 7) times, K4. 63 (71, 79, 87) sts.

Purl 1 row.

Place marker on center st of last row.

Next row (RS): Knit to within 1 st of marked st, M1, K3 (marked st is center st of these 3 sts), M1, knit to end.
Working in St st throughout, cont as follows:
Work 3 rows even.

Rep last 4 rows twice more, then work the inc row again. 71 (79, 87, 95) sts.

Work even until hood measures 6½ (7, 7½, 7¾)" [17 (18, 19, 20) cm] from pick-up row, ending with RS facing for next row.

Next row (RS): Knit to within 2 sts of marked st, K2tog, knit marked st, sl 1, K1, psso, knit to end.
Purl 1 row.
Rep last 2 rows twice more.

Next row (RS): Knit to within 2 sts of marked st, K2tog, knit marked st, sl 1, K1, psso, knit to end.

Next row: Purl to within 2 sts of marked st, P2tog tbl, purl marked st, P2tog, purl to end.
Rep last 2 rows twice more, then work first of these rows again.

Bind off rem 51 (59, 67, 75) sts.

Fold hood in half and join bound-off edges to form top seam of hood.

Front and hood border:
With RS facing, using circular needle and A, and starting and ending at cast-on edges, PU 59 (67, 77, 87) sts up right front opening edge to hood pick-up row, 41 (43, 45, 47) sts up first side of hood to top seam, 41 (43, 45, 47) sts down other side of hood to hood pick-up row, then 59 (67, 77, 87) sts down left front opening edge. 200 (220, 244, 268) sts.

Row 1 (WS): K1, *P2, K2, rep from * to last 3 sts, P2, K1.

Row 2: K3, *P2, K2, rep from * to last st, K1.
These 2 rows form rib patt.
Cont in rib, work as follows:

For a girl only:
Row 3 (buttonhole row) (WS): Rib to last 48 (56, 64, 76) sts, *YO (to make a buttonhole), work 2 tog, rib 9 (11, 13, 16), rep from * 3 times more, YO (to make 5th buttonhole), work 2 tog, rib 2.

For a boy only:
Row 3 (buttonhole row) (WS): Rib 2, *work 2 tog, YO (to make a buttonhole), rib 9 (11, 13, 16), rep from * 3 more times, work 2 tog, YO (to make 5th buttonhole), rib to end.

For both a girl and a boy:
Work in rib patt for 2 more rows, ending with RS facing for next row.
Bind off in rib.

Matching shaped edges at underarm and center of sleeve bound-off edge to shoulder seam, sew sleeves into armholes. Sew side and sleeve seams. Sew on buttons.

Heart sweater

A gorgeous sweater for active little ones, which is also great fun to knit. The heart motif is knitted from a chart, using the intarsia technique. A cool cotton yarn makes the sweater comfortable even on a warm day.

Skill level
Intermediate

Techniques
- Stockinette stitch (page 19)
- Bar increase (page 28)
- Knitting or purling two stitches together (page 31)
- Following a chart (pages 66–67)
- Intarsia (pages 62–63)
- Horizontal stripes (page 60)

Tools
1 pair of US 6 (4 mm) knitting needles
2 stitch holders
Bobbins (see page 15)
Basic equipment for finishing (see page 35)

Materials
Rowan Handknit Cotton 3 (3, 4, 5) balls of 50 g (1¾ oz) yarn in Sugar, 303 (**MC**)

1 (1, 1, 2) balls in Rosso, 215 (**A**)

1 (1, 1, 2) 50 g balls in Ecru, 251 (**B**)

Alternative colors
Variation 1
Decadent, 314 (**MC**)

Lupin, 305 (**A**)

Ecru, 251 (**B**)

Variation 2
Ice Water, 239 (**MC**)

Turkish Plum, 277 (**A**)

Bleached, 263 (**B**)

Gauge
20 sts and 28 rows to 4" (10 cm) measured over St st using US 6 needles. Change needle size if necessary to obtain correct gauge.

Abbreviations
See page 6.

Measurements

Size	1	2	3	4
To fit:	2–3 years	3–4 years	4–5 years	5–6 years
Chest:	20" (51 cm)	22" (56 cm)	24" (61 cm)	26" (66 cm)
Actual measurements				
Chest:	26½" (67 cm)	28¾" (73 cm)	31" (79 cm)	33½" (85 cm)
Length:	11½" (29 cm)	13" (33 cm)	15" (38 cm)	16½" (42 cm)
Sleeve seam:	7" (18 cm)	8¼" (21 cm)	9" (23 cm)	10¼" (26 cm)

Changing colors

When changing color always twist the yarns on the WS of your work, as explained for intarsia (pages 62–63) to avoid leaving a hole.

Back

Using yarn A, cast on 66 (74, 78, 86) sts.
Row 1 (RS): K2, *P2, K2, rep from * to end.
Row 2: P2, *K2, P2, rep from * to end.
These 2 rows form rib patt.
Work in rib for 7 more rows, inc (dec, inc, dec) 1 st at end of last row and ending with WS facing for next row. 67 (73, 79, 85) sts.
Row 10: Purl.
Break off A and join in MC. **
Starting with a knit row, work in St st until back measures 11½ (13, 15, 16½)" [29 (33, 38, 42) cm], ending with RS facing for next row.

Shape shoulders and back neck

Next row (RS): Bind off 18 (20, 22, 24) sts, knit until there are 31 (33, 35, 37) sts on right needle, bind off rem 18 (20, 22, 24) sts.
Break yarn and leave center 31 (33, 35, 37) sts on a holder.

Front

Work as given for back to **.
Starting with a knit row, work in St st for 16 (22, 30, 38) rows, ending with RS facing for next row.
Next row (RS): Using MC, K21 (24, 27, 30), knit next 25 sts as row 1 of chart, reading chart from right to left. Using MC, knit to end.
Next row: Using MC, P21 (24, 27, 30), purl next 25 sts as row 2 of chart, reading chart from left to right. Using MC, purl to end.
These 2 rows set position of chart with side sts in MC.
Cont as set until all 32 rows of chart have been completed.
Starting with a knit row, work in St st until 14 (14, 16, 16) rows fewer have been worked than on back to start of shoulder shaping, ending with RS facing for next row.
Shape neck:
Next row (RS): K27 (29, 32, 34) and turn, leaving rem sts on a holder.
Work each side of neck separately.
Dec 1 st at neck edge of next 8 rows, then on EOR 1 (1, 2, 2) time. 18 (20, 22, 24) sts.
Work 3 rows even, ending with RS facing for next row.
Bind off.
With RS facing, slip center 13 (15, 15, 17) sts onto a

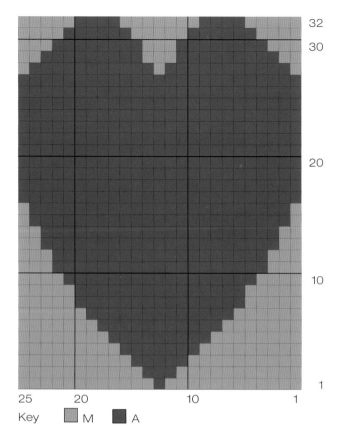

Key ☐ M ■ A

holder, rejoin yarn to rem sts, knit to end.
Complete to match first side, reversing shaping.

Sleeves

Using MC, cast on 30 (30, 34, 34) sts.
Work in rib patt as given for back for 6 rows.
Join in B.
Using B, work in rib for 2 more rows, inc 0 (1, 0, 1) sts at each end of last row and ending with RS facing for next row. 30 (32, 34, 36) sts.
Starting with a knit row, work in St st throughout as follows:
Using B, work 4 rows, inc 1 st at each end of 3rd row. 32 (34, 36, 38) sts.
Using MC, work 6 rows, inc 1 st at each end of next row and EOR 2 (2, 2, 1) times. 38 (40, 42, 42) sts.
Using B, work 6 rows, inc 1 st at each end of next (3rd, next, next) and foll alt (0, 4th, 4th) row. 42 (42, 46, 46) sts.
Last 12 rows form striped St st patt.
Cont in striped St st patt, shaping sides by inc 1 st at each end of next (next, 3rd, 3rd) row and then every 4th row until there are 52 (56, 60, 64) sts.
Work even until sleeve measures 7 (8¼, 9, 10¼)" [18 (21, 23, 26) cm], ending with WS row.
Bind off on RS.

To finish

Press carefully following instructions on yarn label. Sew right shoulder seam.

Neckband:

With RS facing and using A, PU 13 (13, 14, 14) sts down left side of neck, knit across 13 (15, 15, 17) sts from front holder, PU 13 (13, 14, 14) sts up right side of neck, and then knit across 31 (33, 35, 37) sts from back holder. 70 (74, 78, 82) sts.

Starting with row 2 of rib patt, work in rib as given for back for 6 (6, 8, 8) rows, ending with WS facing for next row.

Bind off in rib (on WS).

Sew left shoulder and neckband seam. Mark points along side seam edges 5 (5½, 6, 6¼)" [13 (14, 15, 16) cm] to either side of shoulder seams and sew bound-off edge of sleeves to body between these points. Weave in loose ends. Sew side and underarm seams.

Winter scarf and mittens

This cozy scarf and mittens set will keep little hands and necks nice and snug, on chilly winter days.

Skill level
Challenging

Techniques
- Stockinette stitch (page 19)
- Horizontal stripes (page 60)
- Stranding yarns (page 64)
- Following a chart (pages 66–67)
- Bar increase (page 28)
- Picking up stitches (page 33)
- Knitting two stitches together (page 31)
- Knitting two stitches together "tbl" (page 31)
- Making 1 increase (page 29)

Tools
1 pair of US 6 (4 mm) knitting needles
Basic equipment for finishing (see page 35)

Materials
Rowan Wool Cotton
3 balls of 50 g (1¾ oz) yarn in Antique, 900 (**A**)

1 ball in Bilberry Fool, 959 (**B**)

1 ball in Hiss, 952 (**C**)

Alternative colors
Variation 1
Antique, 900 (**A**)

Aloof, 958 (**B**)

Citron, 901 (**C**)

Variation 2
Clear, 941 (**A**)

Aloof, 958 (**B**)

Ship Shape, 955 (**C**)

Gauge
22 sts and 30 rows to 4" (10 cm) measured over St st using US 6 needles. Change needle size if necessary to obtain correct gauge.

Abbreviations
See page 6.

Changing colors
When changing color on scarf, break off and rejoin yarns, leaving ends long enough for weaving in later. For mittens, yarns can be carried up the side of the work.

Measurements

Size	1	2
To fit:	1–2 years	3–4 years
Mittens:	5½" × 5" (14 × 12.5 cm)	6" × 5½" (15 × 14 cm)
Scarf:	8" × 46" (20 × 117 cm) (one size)	

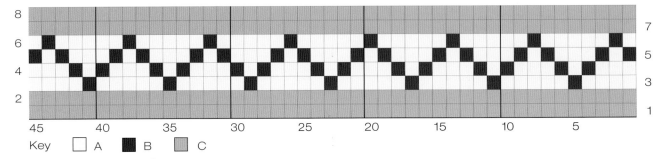

8
6
4
2

7
5
3
1

45   40   35   30   25   20   15   10   5

Key ☐ A ■ B ▨ C

Scarf

Using yarn B, cast on 45 sts.
Row 1: K3, *P3, K3, rep from * to end.
Row 2: P3, *K3, P3, rep from * to end.
These 2 rows form rib patt.
Change to C. Work 2 rows in rib.
Change to A. Work 2 rows in rib.
Change to B. Work 2 rows in rib.
Change to C. Work 2 rows in rib.
Change to A. Work 2 rows in rib.
Next row: Knit.
Next row: Purl.
These 2 rows form St st.
Work 6 more rows in St st.
Cont in St st, **work 8 rows from Chart.
Change to A. Work 8 rows in St st.
Change to C. Work 2 rows in St st.
Change to A. Work 2 rows in St st.
Change to B. Work 2 rows in St st.
Change to A. Work 2 rows in St st.
Change to C. Work 2 rows in St st.

Change to A. Work 2 rows in St st.
Change to B. Work 2 rows in St st.
Change to A. Work 8 rows in St st.**
The 38 rows from ** to ** form patt.
Cont in patt until scarf measures approx 42" (110 cm),
finishing with patt from chart.
Change to A. Work 8 rows in St st.
Rib 2 rows A, C, B, A, C and B.
Bind off in rib using B.

Right mitten

**Using yarn B, cast on 30 (34) sts.
Row 1: K2, * P2, K2, rep from * to end.
Row 2: P2, * K2, P2, rep from * to end.
These 2 rows form rib patt.
Change to C.
Work 2 rows in rib.
Change to A.
Work 2 rows in rib.
Work the last 6 rows once more.
Next row (RS): Knit.

Next row: Purl.

These 2 rows form St st.

Work 2 more rows in St st for second size only.**

Shape thumb:

Row 1 (RS): K16 (17), M1, K1 (3), M1, K13 (14).

Work 1 (3) rows in St st.

Next row: K16 (17), M1, K3 (5), M1, K13 (14).

Next row: Purl.

Cont to inc as before on next 2 RS rows.

38 (42) sts.

Next row: Purl.

Knit thumb:

Next row (RS): K 25(28), turn.

Next row: P 9 (11), turn.

***Working on these 9 (11) sts , work 8 (10) rows in St st.

Next row: K1, (K2tog) to end.

Break off yarn and thread through rem sts. Pull tight and fasten off.

Sew thumb seam.

With RS facing, rejoin A to base of thumb and PU 2 sts at base of thumb, then knit to end. 31 (33) sts.

Next row: Purl.

Change to C.

Work 2 rows in St st.

Change to yarns A and B.

Next row: K3 (4) in A, K1 in B, *K5 in A, K1 in B, rep from * to last 3 (4) sts, K3 (4) sts in A.

Next row: P2 (3) in A, P1 in B, P1 in A, P1 in B, *P3 in A, P1 in B, P1 in A, P1 in B, rep from * to last 2 (3) sts, P2 (3) in A.

Next row: K1 (2) in A, K1 in B, K3 in A,* K1 in B, K1 in A, K1 in B, K3 in A, rep from * to last 2 (3) sts, K1 in B, K1 (2) in A.

Next row: P0 (1) in A, P1 in B, *P5 in A, P1 in B, rep from * to last 0 (1) sts, P0 (1) in A.

Work 2 rows in St st in C.

Change to A.

Next row (RS): K1, (K2tog tbl, K10 [11], K2tog, K1) twice. 27 (29) sts.

Next row: Purl.

Next row: K1, (K2tog tbl, K 8 [9], K2tog, K1) twice. 23 (25) sts.

Next row: Purl.

Next row: K1, (K2tog tbl, K6 [7], K2tog, K1) twice. 19 (21) sts.

Bind off.

Left mitten

Work as for right mitten from ** to **.

Shape thumb:

Row 1 (RS): K13 (14), M1, K1 (3), M1, K16 (17).

Work 1 (3) rows in St st.

Next row: K13 (14), M1, K3 (5), M1, K16 (17).

Next row: Purl.

Cont to inc as before on next 2 RS rows.

38 (42) sts.

Next row: Purl.

Knit thumb:

Next row (RS): K22 (25), turn.

Next row: P9 (11), turn.

Work from *** to end as for right mitten.

To finish

Block scarf or press lightly, following instructions on yarn label. Weave in loose ends.

Block mittens. Weave in loose ends. Sew seams using backstitch or an edge-to-edge seam.

Tassel hat

This droll two-color hat, with its perky tassels, is sure to look great on little ones. And, as there is no shaping to do, it is very simple to make!

Skill level
Easy

Techniques
- Stockinette stitch (page 19)
- Seed stitch (page 168)
- Weaving in ends (page 37)
- Seams (page 36)
- Tassels (page 75)

Tools
1 pair of US 3 (3.25 mm) knitting needles
1 pair of US 5 (3.75 mm) knitting needles
Basic equipment for finishing (see page 35)

Materials
 Jaeger Matchmaker Merino DK
1 ball of 50 g (1¾ oz) yarn in Rosy, 870 (**A**)

1 ball in Petal, 883 (**B**)

Alternative colors
 Mariner, 629 **A**

 Feather, 864 **B**

Gauge
23 sts and 30 rows to 4" (10 cm) measured over St st using US 5 needles. Change needle size if necessary to obtain correct gauge.

Abbreviations
See page 6.

Hat
Using larger needles and A, cast on 49 (53, 57) sts.
Row 1 (RS): K1, *P1, K1, rep from * to end.
Row 2: P1, *K1, P1, rep from * to end.
These 2 rows form seed st patt.
Work in seed st for 16 (19, 19) more rows.
Change to smaller needles.
Work in seed st for 18 (21, 21) rows, ending with RS facing for next row.
Break off A and join in B.

Change to larger needles.
Starting with a knit row, work in St st until Hat measures 11¾ (13¾, 15¼)" [30 (35, 39) cm], ending with RS row.
Break off B and join in A.
Change to smaller needles.
Next row (WS): Purl.
Work in seed st for 18 (21, 21) rows.
Change to larger needles.
Work in seed st for 18 (21, 21) more rows, ending with WS row.
Bind off in seed st on RS.

To finish
Press carefully following instructions on yarn label. Weave in loose ends.
Fold hat in half, matching cast-on and bound-off edges, and sew side seams, reversing seam for section in B for brim. Fold brim to outside.
Using A, make two 3" (8 cm)-long tassels and sew to corners of hat as shown in photograph.

Measurements

Size	1	2	3
To fit:	1–2 years	3–4 years	5–6 years
Actual measurements			
Around head:	43 cm (17")	46 cm (18")	50 cm (19½")

God wants us to take care of the gifts of the land.

God does not want us to waste his gifts.
How can we care for God's gifts?

Match each square with a way you can care.

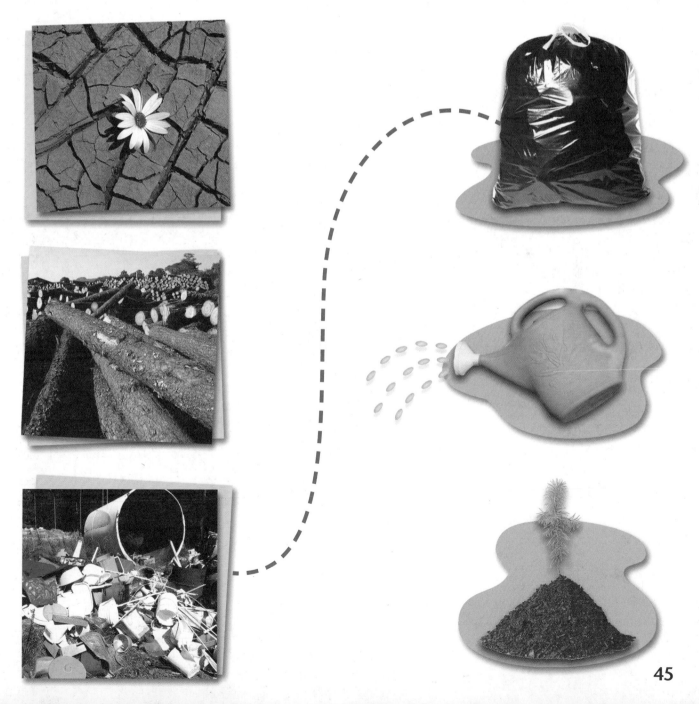

45

WE RESPOND

How can we share God's gifts?

Talk about each picture.

Saint Rose of Lima

Long ago, in Lima, Peru, there lived a young girl named Isabelle.

People said she was as pretty as a rose. So her family began to call her Rose.

Fold

Many poor people came to Rose's home for help. She took care of the poor and sick. She spent every day sharing God's love.

Rose wanted to help her own poor family. She planted a flower garden. She sold the flowers she grew.

Fold

Rose loved God very much. Rose loved all people.

Let's Celebrate
God's Gift of Land

✝ **We Pray**

For ⛰, we thank you, God.

For 🌵, we thank you, God.

For 🫐, we thank you, God.

For 🌲, we thank you, God.

For the land and all that fills it, we thank you, God.

The world is made of land and water.

Color the spaces with L  green .

Color the spaces with W blue .

Add stars, the sun, and the moon.

Take Home

Try to put the words *reduce*, *reuse*, and *recycle* into action in your home by making less trash, creatively reusing items that would otherwise be thrown away, and recycling those items that must be.

God Made the Animals

WE GATHER

Genesis 1:25

God made all kinds of animals. "God saw how good it was."

What is your favorite animal?

51

God made all kinds of animals.

God loves us.
God cares for us.
God filled the world with animals.

Pretend you are your favorite animal.
Let your friends guess what you are.

Draw your favorite animal.
Could you take care of this animal?
How?

53

How can you thank
God for animals?
Taking care of them is
one way to thank him.

🧍 Circle ways to take
care of animals.

A Special Blessing

Next week is the Feast of Saint Francis. He shared God's love with everyone.

Fold

This is what Saint Francis did. He blessed all the animals.

4

Let's Celebrate

God's Gift of Animals

✝ **We Pray**

🎵 **God Made All the Animals**

("Here We Go 'Round the Mulberry Bush")

God made all the animals,
The animals, the animals.
God made all the animals
God made our animal friends.

Have you seen an elephant walk?
An elephant walk, an elephant walk?
Have you seen an elephant walk?
God made this animal friend.

Have you heard a lion roar?
A lion roar, a lion roar?
Have you heard a lion roar?
God made this animal friend.

Pray
Learn
Celebrate
Share
Choose
Live

Read the story.

 has a  .

 walks the 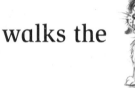 with a  .

 throws a to the  .

washes the  in the  .

 gives the  food and water .

How would you care for a pet?

Take Home

Find children's books at the library or bookstore that help your family to learn about caring for animals.

The Church Year

Advent | Christmas | Ordinary Time | Lent | Three Days | Easter | Ordinary Time

WE GATHER

📖 Psalm 98:4

"Shout with joy to the LORD,
    all the earth;
    break into song; sing praise."

What do you like to do when you celebrate?

59

God wants us to celebrate his love for us.

We celebrate God's love in many ways.
We pray to him with our families.
We sing to him with our friends.

Draw yourself celebrating.

We celebrate the Church year.

We celebrate God's love all year.
We have special times of celebration.
These times help us to remember
God's love.

🏃 Act out some ways we
celebrate God's love.

♫ Make a Joyful Noise

Chorus
Make a joyful noise to our God on high!
  Make a joyful noise to our God!

Praise God with the trumpet blast,
  praise God with the cymbal crash.
Praise God with a joyful dance,
  praise the name of our God! (Chorus)
Praise God with the strings and reed,
  praise God with your melodies.
Praise God with a symphony,
  praise the name of our God! (Chorus)

We Celebrate All Year

We use God's gifts when we celebrate.

Fold

God's gifts help us to remember his love. They help us to celebrate all year long.

We use water
and light.

Fold

We use flowers
and plants, too.

Let's Celebrate
All Year

✝ **We Pray**

Leader: We celebrate when it's sunny.

All: Praise God!

Leader: We celebrate when it's snowy.

All: Praise God!

Leader: We celebrate when the flowers bloom.

All: Praise God!

Leader: We celebrate when the leaves are falling.

All: Praise God!

Leader: We celebrate all year long!

All: Praise God!

PROJECT DISCIPLE

Draw a ✔ next to the ways to celebrate God's love.

Take Home

Your family can celebrate God's love together. Find some ways to do this each day!

Ordinary Time

Advent | Christmas | Ordinary Time | Lent | Three Days | Easter | Ordinary Time

WE GATHER

Mark 12:30

Love God with all your heart, with all your mind, and with all your strength. Love your neighbor as yourself.

What person do you know who takes special care of everyone?

67

All during the year we celebrate Jesus' love.

Jesus had many friends.
They celebrated his love.
They tried to be like him.

Jesus' friends lived
their lives loving God.
They are
called saints.

Saint Peter was one of
Jesus' first friends.
He told many people
about Jesus.

Saint Patrick was a
bishop in Ireland.
He taught the people
there about God.

We celebrate Ordinary Time.

Saints always tried to share God's love with others.

Saint Martin de Porres lived in Peru. He took care of people who were poor and hungry.

Saint Katharine Drexel lived in the United States. She taught children about Jesus.

WE RESPOND

We are called to be saints, too.
We do this by loving God and loving others.
What can you do to show love for God?
What can you do to show love for others?

Draw yourself here and write your name under your picture.

Saint Joseph

Joseph was a good man. He lived in Nazareth with Mary and Jesus.

Joseph is a saint.

Saint Joseph

4

Joseph loved God very much. Joseph cared for Mary and Jesus.

Fold

Joseph showed God his love by the things he said and did.

Let's Celebrate
The Saints

✝ **We Pray**

🎵 **When the Saints Go Marching In**

Oh, when the saints go marching in,
Oh, when the saints go marching in,
O Lord, I want to be in that number,
When the saints go marching in.

Tell what is happening in each picture.

Color the ♡ under the picture that shows
the children showing love for others.

Take Home

Find out if anyone in your family is named for a saint.
If so, learn about the saint together.

God Is Our Creator

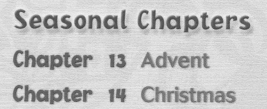

Seasonal Chapters

DEAR FAMILY

Pray Learn Celebrate Share Choose Live

In Unit 2 your child will grow as a disciple of Jesus by:

- learning that God our Creator made and loves all people
- using the senses God gave us to discover God's world
- seeing the ways we can learn about God in our families
- sharing God's love by caring for our families and friends
- celebrating all of God's gifts in prayer.

Question Corner

Each of us experiences the world through God's gift of our senses. Together, ask your family members and friends which of the senses is most important to them and why. Talk with your child about people who cannot see or cannot hear and ways we can show respect for them.

Make it Happen

We all learn about God with our families and friends. Talk with your child about the people who have helped you to learn about God and what they taught you. Ask your child to share one thing they have learned about God with a family member or friend.

Show That You Care

Together discuss family members, friends, or neighbors who are having difficulties—for example illness or job loss—and who may need a reminder of God's love. Make a *God loves you!* sign for one or some of those people. Send it by mail or, if possible, deliver it together.

Pray Today

Together make a list of all the people who are important to your family. Have your child decorate the list and display it where you say nighttime prayers. Ask God to bless all the people on your list.

Reality Check

"Parents must regard their children as *children of God* and respect them as *human persons*."

(*Catechism of the Catholic Church*, 2222)

Take Home

Each chapter in your child's *We Believe* Kindergarten text offers a "Take Home" activity that invites your family to support your child's journey to more fully become a disciple of Christ.

Be ready for this unit's Take Home:

Chapter 8: Learning about your family's heritage

Chapter 9: Celebrating family members' unique traits

Chapter 10: Planning a family dinner that celebrates the senses

Chapter 11: Sharing God's love as a family

Chapter 12: Thanking God for family friends

God Made All People

WE GATHER

📖 Acts of the Apostles 17:25

God "gives to everyone life and breath and everything."

What would you like to ask the people in these pictures?

77

God made everyone.

God made all people good.
God gave people many gifts.
He gave people the world and
all the good things in it.

Add people to this picture.
Show them enjoying God's world.

WE BELIEVE

God loves all people.

There are people in every
part of the world.
God loves all of them.
He wants them to love him.
God wants all people
to share his love.

Add yourself in the picture.

WE RESPOND

Cut out the hearts at the side of the page. Look at each picture. Talk about the way people are sharing God's love. If this is a way you can share love, put a heart near the picture.

The People We See

Here are people wearing different kinds of clothes.

Who made these people?

God made all people.

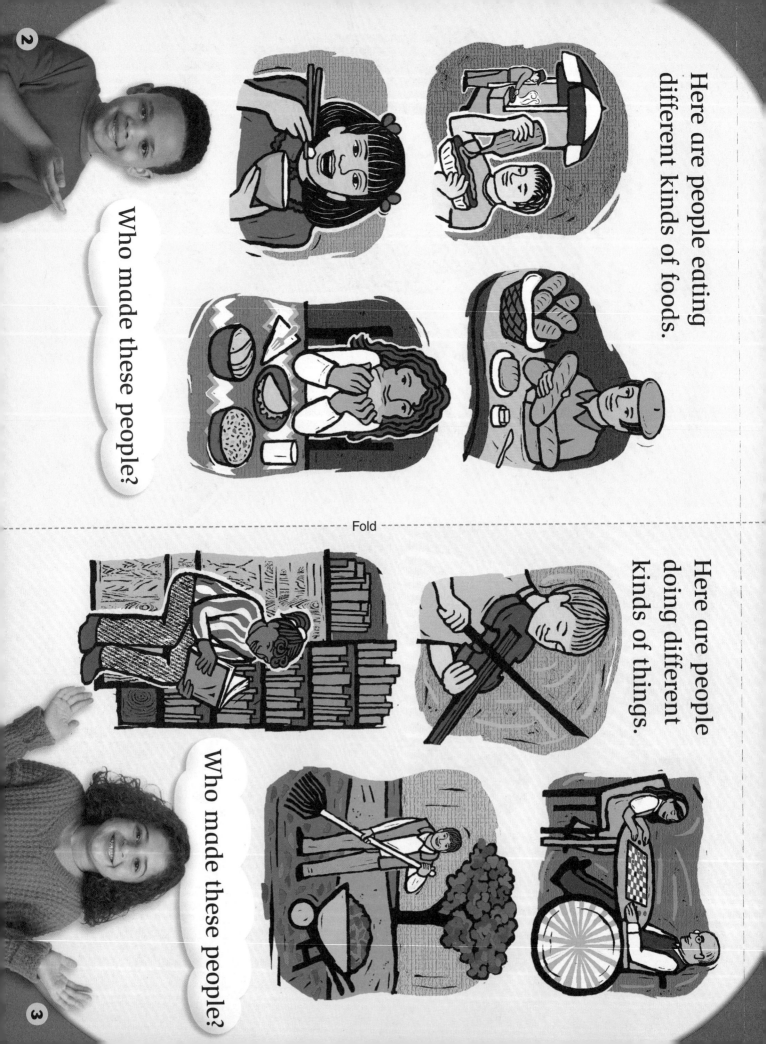

Here are people eating different kinds of foods.

Who made these people?

Here are people doing different kinds of things.

Who made these people?

2

3

Let's Celebrate
God's Gift of People

✝ We Pray

♫ God Made People

("Here We Go 'Round the Mulberry Bush")

God made people out of love,
out of love, out of love.
God made people out of love.
Let's join our hands and thank him.

God wants us to share his love,
share his love, share his love.
God wants us to share his love.
Let's all shake hands and thank him.

PROJECT DISCIPLE

 Pray Learn Celebrate Share Choose Live

Finish the prayer with pictures.

God, you made

Thank you for loving

I want to share your love with

Amen.

www.webelieveweb.com

Take Home

Share family stories, interview relatives, and spark curiosity about your family's heritage.

84 Kindergarten Chapter 8

God Made Us

9

WE GATHER

📖 Psalm 139:14

God, "I praise you, so wonderfully you made me."

Imagine you are meeting someone for the first time. Tell this person about yourself.

WE BELIEVE

God made you.

God made you special.
There is no other person exactly like you.

🏃 Here I am.

My name is

God loves you.

God loves you just the way you are.
God never stops loving you.

GOD LOVES ME!

Color this important message.
Remember it always.

We thank God for his love.
We can tell God we love him.

In sign language,

is the sign for **I love you.**

Make this sign with your hand.
Raise it above your head to say,
"I love you, God."

You Can Tell God Anything

You can talk to God anytime.
You can tell God anything.

God, this is my favorite color.

God, this is a picture of my favorite story.

God, this is my favorite food.

Fold

God, this is my favorite toy or game.

Let's Celebrate
God's Gift of Me

✟ **We Pray**

🎵 **I Know That God Loves Me**

From the top of my head,
from the top of my head,
To the ends of my toes,
to the ends of my toes,
I know that God loves me.
(Repeat)

I know, I know, I know, I know,
I know that God loves me.

From my fingertips,
from my fingertips,
To the smile on my lips,
to the smile on my lips,
I know that God loves me.
(Repeat)

I know, I know, I know, I know,
I know that God loves me.

PROJECT DISCIPLE

Pray
Learn
Celebrate
Share
Choose
Live

Tell about yourself by circling your choices.

Which is your favorite color?

blue   green   red

orange   yellow   purple

Which is your favorite activity?

Which is your favorite season?

Share your choices with a friend.

Take Home

Family members may share certain traits and characteristics but each person is unique. Celebrate this by pointing out unique traits in each other in positive ways.

God Helps Us to Discover

WE GATHER

Psalm 63:5

God, "I will lift up my hands, calling on your name."

What are these children discovering about God's world?

WE BELIEVE

God gives us our senses.

God gives us the gift of our senses.

🧍 Which senses would you use to enjoy each gift from God?

Match.

see

hear

taste

smell

touch

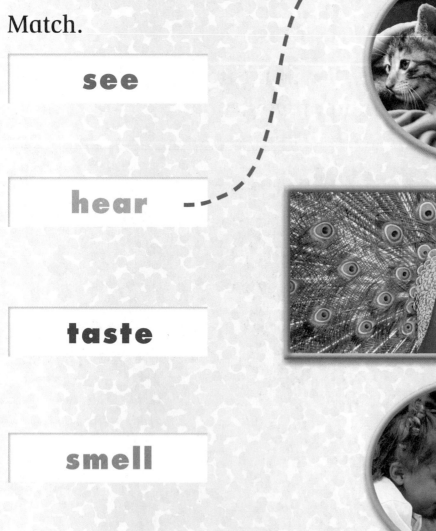

We use our senses to discover God's world.

Go on a discovery walk.
Find out more about God's world.

 Draw things you see, hear, touch, taste, and smell.

95

WE RESPOND

🎵 **God Gave Me My Senses**
(*"Mary Had a Little Lamb"*)

God gave me my 👂👂 to hear,

ears to hear, ears to hear.

God gave me my 👂👂 to hear,

and this is what I hear. (Tell what you hear.)

Add these verses.

- God gave me my 👄 to taste.
- God gave me my 👁 👁 to see.
- God gave me my 👃 to smell.

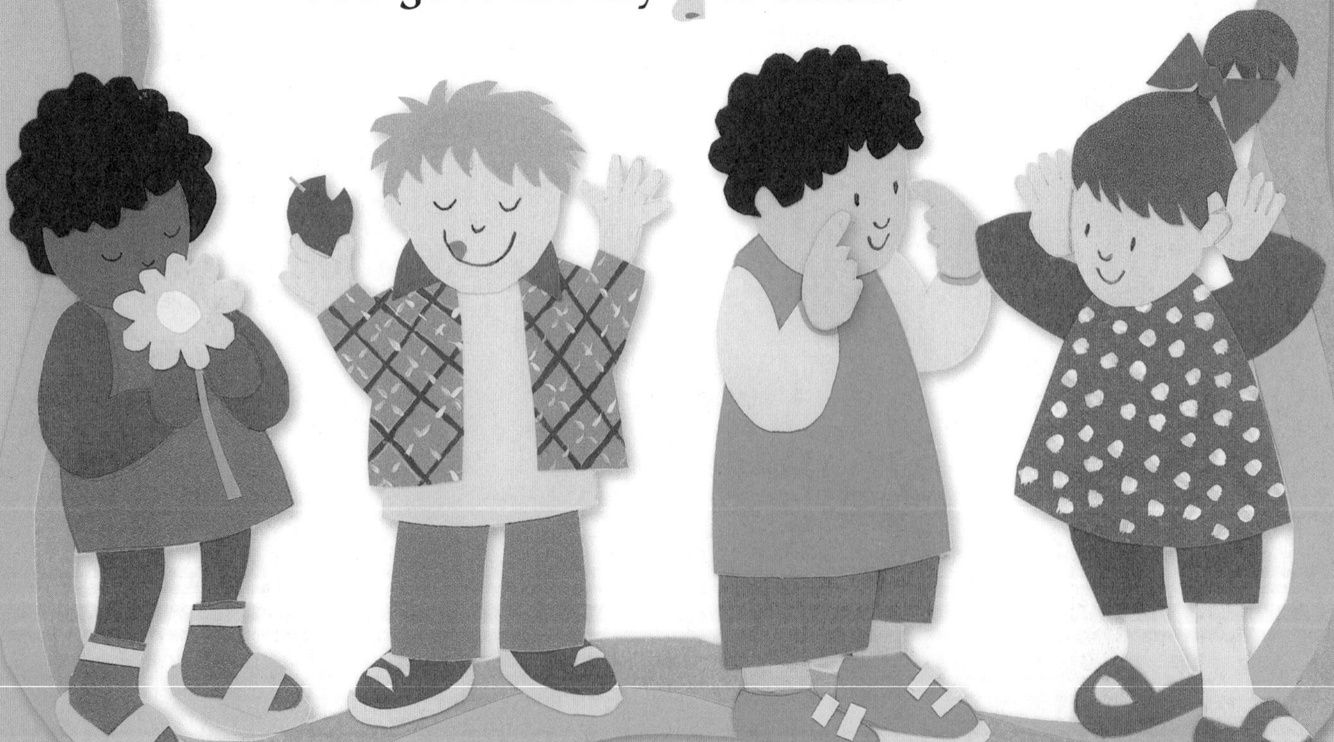

God's Gifts— My Senses

I use my senses to enjoy God's world.

I use my senses to show my love for God.

Fold

I use my senses to learn.

Fold

I use my senses to show love for myself and others.

Welcome

Let's Celebrate
Our Senses

✝ **We Pray**

God, help me to use my senses to discover more about your world.

Leader: God, bless my eyes.

All: They help me to discover more about your world.

- God, bless my ears. (All)
- God, bless my nose. (All)
- God, bless my mouth. (All)
- God, bless my hands. (All)

PROJECT DISCIPLE

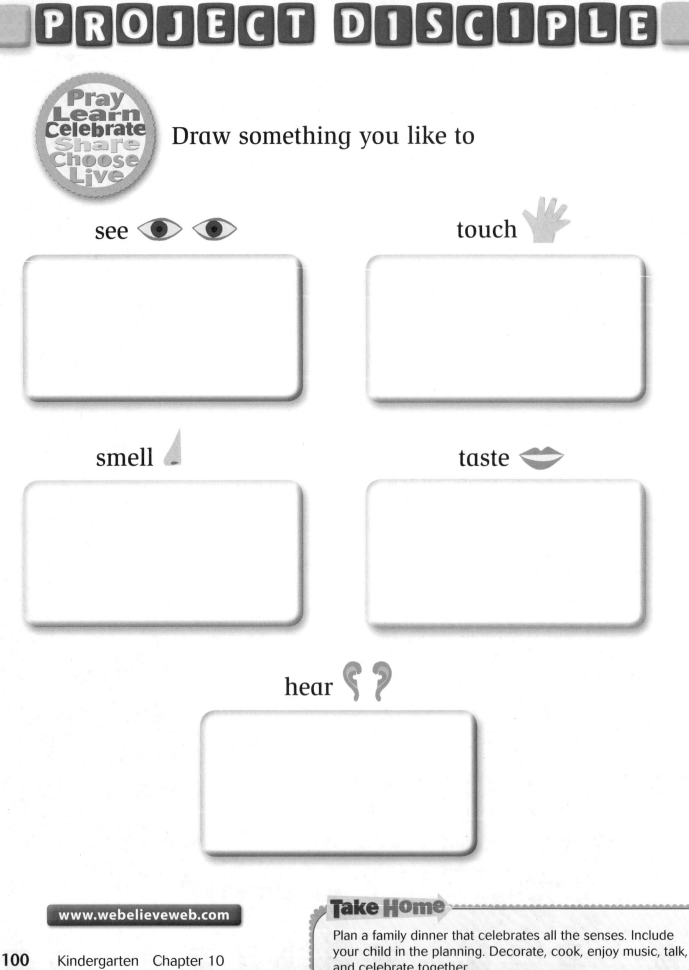

Pray Learn Celebrate Share Choose Live

Draw something you like to

see 👀

touch ✋

smell 👃

taste 👄

hear 👂👂

Take Home

Plan a family dinner that celebrates all the senses. Include your child in the planning. Decorate, cook, enjoy music, talk, and celebrate together.

We Learn About God with Our Families

11

WE GATHER

📖 Psalm 136:1

Praise God, who is so good,
God's love lasts forever.

Where do you think this family is going?
Where do you like to go with your family?

Our families help us to discover God's world.

God wants families to spend time together.

Talk about each picture. What is the family discovering about God's world?

 Circle the pictures that show things you like to do with your family.

What else do families like to do together?

WE BELIEVE

Our families share God's love.

Our families show us God's love.

🏃 Match.

Families keep us safe.

Families teach us to share.

Families care for others.

Families talk things over with us.

103

WE RESPOND

We do things with our family
to share God's love.
We do things for our family
to share God's love.

Show how your family can
share God's love.

Draw a picture of your family.

Share your picture with your family.

God Cares for Our Families

📖 Psalm 23

The Lord is our shepherd.
He takes care of us.

Fold

God's love will always be with us.

2

God shows us the way to be good.

Fold

3

God watches over us. He helps us to be safe.

Let's Celebrate
God's Gift of Our Families

✟ We Pray

All: God, help us share your love.

Leader:
- With our family, (All)

- With our mothers, fathers, brothers, and sisters, (All)

- With our grandparents, aunts, uncles, and cousins, (All)

- With our godparents and friends, (All)

- With all people, (All)

Ices

PROJECT DISCIPLE

Pray
Learn
Celebrate
Share
Choose
Live

Listen to the story. Color the picture.

Read to Me

Saint Gianna shared God's love with others.

Saint Gianna was a daughter and sister.
She shared God's love with her family.

Saint Gianna was a mother.
She shared God's love with her children.

Saint Gianna was a doctor.
She shared God's love with her patients.

www.webelieveweb.com

Take Home

Whenever your family shows it cares, or shares with others,
remember and remind each other that you are sharing
God's love.

We Learn About God with Our Friends

12

WE GATHER

📖 Psalm 150:6

"Let everything that has breath give praise to the LORD!"

Why do you like to be with your friends?

Friends are special gifts from God.

Together we can discover God's world.
We can talk with each other.
We can listen and learn.
We can help each other.

🧍 Draw a picture of
your special friends.

We show our friends God's love.

Friends can show God's love every day.

Which picture shows friends sharing with each other? Draw a ▢ by it.

Which picture shows friends helping each other? Draw a △ by it.

Which picture shows friends helping other people? Draw a ⬤ by it.

WE RESPOND

Friends can share God's love. Friends can help each other.

Find the path to the Good Friends' Garden. Talk about the pictures that are on that path.

Good Friends' Garden

START

POPCORN

MUD

FRIENDS WITH GOD

Saints are friends of God.
Saints are our friends, too.
Saints help us to learn
about God.
I can name some saints.
Can you?

BOOK OF SAINTS

Saint Thérèse of Lisieux
was a friend of God.
She helped people all
over the world.
She prayed for them.

Saint Frances of Rome
was a friend of God.
She helped hungry people.
She gave them food.

Fold

Saint Martin de Porres
was a friend of God.
He helped sick people.
He cared for them.

Let's Celebrate
Friends

✞ **We Pray**

🎵 **The Gifts of God's Love**
("Did You Ever See a Lassie?")

Let's celebrate together,
together, together.
Let's celebrate together
God's great love for us.

God gives us our families.
He gives us our good friends.
Let's celebrate together
The gifts of God's love.

PROJECT DISCIPLE

Pray Learn Celebrate Share Choose Live

Tell what is happening in each picture.

Color the ♡ over the picture of the children showing God's love.

www.webelieveweb.com

Take Home

Think about your family's friends and the times you share. Thank God for these special people and times.

116   Kindergarten   Chapter 12

Advent

Advent | Christmas | Ordinary Time | Lent | Three Days | Easter | Ordinary Time

WE GATHER

Come, Lord Jesus!

How do you wait for someone special?

God gives us the greatest gift.

God sent his Son to the world.
God's Son would share his love with everyone.

God's Son would be the Light of the World.
To help you remember, finish this sun.
Cut out small pieces of yellow and orange paper.
Put paste on the empty spaces.
Then put the colored paper on these spaces.

We celebrate Advent.

God chose Mary to be the Mother
of his Son.
Mary and her husband, Joseph,
waited for the Son of God to be born.
They would name him Jesus.

Trace over the dots.
Show how Mary and Joseph are
getting ready for Jesus.

WE RESPOND

We get ready to celebrate the coming
of the Son of God.
We get ready by sharing and caring.

Draw a picture in each box.
Show how you will share and care.

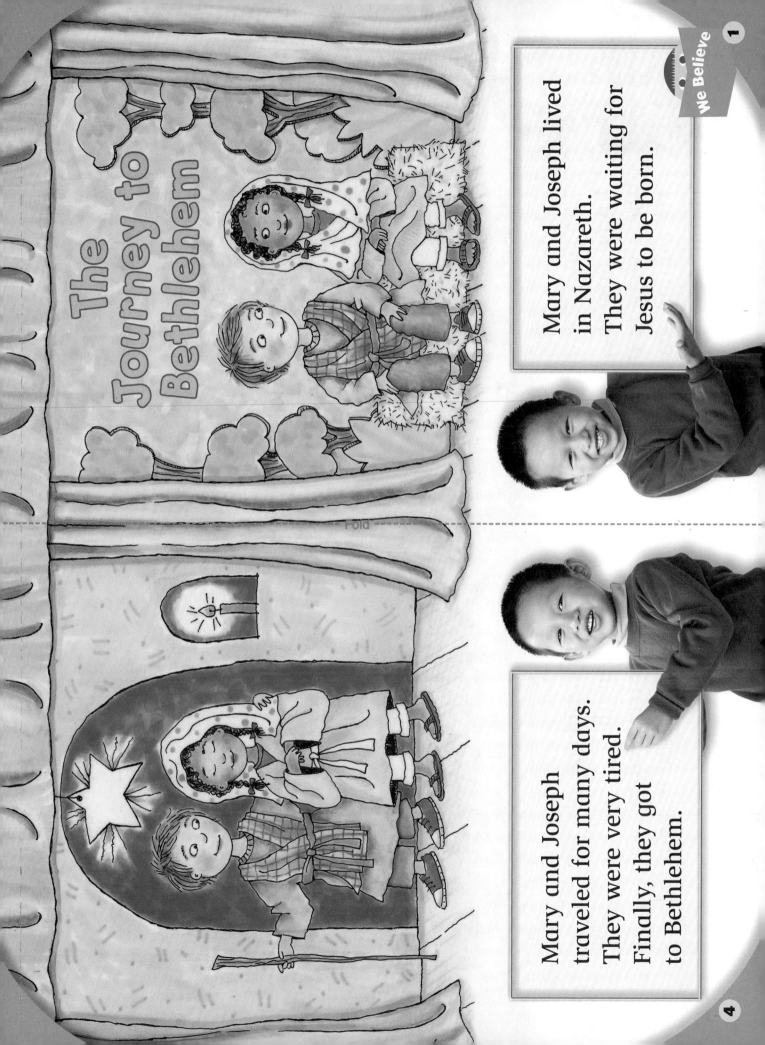

The Journey to Bethlehem

Mary and Joseph lived
in Nazareth.
They were waiting for
Jesus to be born.

Mary and Joseph
traveled for many days.
They were very tired.
Finally, they got
to Bethlehem.

Fold

The ruler wanted to know how many people there were in the world. He wanted everyone counted.

Mary and Joseph left Nazareth. They traveled to Bethlehem to be counted.

Let's Celebrate
Waiting for Jesus

✝ **We Pray**

🎵 **Advent Canon**

Come, Lord Jesus,
come and save us.
Come, Lord Jesus, come.

In this season
we are waiting.
Come, Lord Jesus, come.

PROJECT DISCIPLE

Help Mary and Joseph find their way from Nazareth to Bethlehem.

Take Home

Commemorate Advent as a family by displaying an Advent calendar. Open a door of the calendar together each day as you pray, *Come, Lord Jesus.*

Christmas

14

WE GATHER

Isaiah 9:5

"For a child is born to us,
a son is given us."

What are some special gifts
God has given to us?

Jesus was born in Bethlehem.

📖 Luke 2:1–8

Read to Me

When Mary and Joseph reached Bethlehem, they were very tired. There was no place to stay. Finally an innkeeper let them stay in the place where he kept his animals. Jesus was born there. Mary wrapped him in a cloth. She laid him in a manger that was filled with hay.

🎵 Away in a Manger

Away in a manger,
no crib for a bed,
The little Lord Jesus
laid down his
sweet head;
The stars in the sky
looked down
where he lay,
The little Lord Jesus,
asleep on the hay.

We celebrate Christmas.

Each Christmas we celebrate the birth of Jesus.
All over the world people pray and thank God for sending his Son.

Make a "Star of Bethlehem." It will be like the bright one in the sky on the night Jesus was born.

Rejoice! Jesus is born!
We welcome you, Jesus,
each in our own way.

Talk about some special things your family does for Christmas. Draw one of them here.

The Visit of the Shepherds

It was the night Jesus was born.

The shepherds went to Bethlehem to find Jesus. The shepherds were happy to find the newborn baby.

Shepherds were in a
field near Bethlehem.
They were taking care
of their sheep.

Suddenly, a bright light lit up
the sky.
Angels started to sing.
The angels told the shepherds
about Jesus.

Let's Celebrate
Christmas

✝ **We Pray**

♫ **Silent Night, Holy Night**

Silent night! Holy night!
All is calm, all is bright
Round yon Virgin Mother
and child!
Holy infant so tender and mild,
Sleep in heavenly peace,
Sleep in heavenly peace.

Silent night! Holy night!
Shepherds quake at the sight;
Glories stream from heaven afar;
Heav'nly hosts sing "Alleluia!
Christ the Savior is born,
Christ the Savior is born."

PROJECT DISCIPLE

Pray
Learn
Celebrate
Share
Choose
Live

Circle the ways you can celebrate Christmas.

Take Home

What can your family learn from the many Christmas hymns about Jesus' birth?

Jesus Shows Us God's Love

UNIT 3

Seasonal Chapters

In Unit 3 your child will grow as a disciple of Jesus by:

- appreciating Mary's role in God's plan
- understanding that God the Father showed his love by sending Jesus
- learning about the Holy Family and praying to them
- listening to Jesus' teachings
- being kind, good, caring, and loving as Jesus was.

What Would you do?

Jesus wants us to show others that we love them. Decide on one way your family will show love for:

Neighbors _____

People in your parish _____

Workers _____

Each other _____

Pray Today

One way we can honor Mary is by praying to her. The Hail Mary is on page 141 of your child's text. Ask your child to teach the prayer gestures to your family. Pray the Hail Mary as a family each day for a week.

Reality Check

"The Christian family is a communion of persons, a sign and image of the communion of the Father and the Son in the Holy Spirit."

(*Catechism of the Catholic Church*, 2205)

What's the Word?

Ask your child to share what he or she is learning about Jesus and his teachings. Then invite each family member to share a favorite Scripture story of Jesus. You might refer to a children's Bible as each person shares his or her favorite.

More to Explore

As your child learns about Jesus and his family, use a globe or world map to find the places Jesus lived or visited. Look for Bethlehem, Nazareth, and Jerusalem. Then choose one of these cities to research further and discover what that place is like today.

Take Home

Each chapter in your child's *We Believe* Kindergarten text offers a "Take Home" activity that invites your family to support your child's journey to more fully become a disciple of Christ.

Be ready for this unit's Take Home:

Chapter 15: Honoring Mary at home and church

Chapter 16: Learning about Jesus in the Bible

Chapter 17: Comparing your own family with the Holy Family

Chapter 18: Acting like Jesus

Chapter 19: Sharing love as a family

God Chooses Mary

WE GATHER

📖 Luke 1:28

God is with you.

Michael Escoffery, *A Child Is Born*

Martin and his dad are looking at a special picture.

What does the picture show?

135

Mary loved God very much.

There was a young Jewish
girl named Mary.
She lived with her family
in the town of Nazareth.
Mary showed her love for God.
She helped other people.
Mary prayed every day.

How do you think Mary helped
her mother? Act it out.

God asked Mary to be the Mother of his Son.

📖 Luke 1:26–31

Read Along

One day an angel brought Mary a message from God. God wanted Mary to be the Mother of his Son. God wanted her to name the child Jesus.

Mary wanted to do what God asked.

What did Mary say to God?

Mary's answer to God is hiding in these letters.

🏃 Circle it.

M G Y E S D Q

WE RESPOND

We can show our love for God, too.
This is how we say **yes** to God.
We can pray.
We can work and play together.
We can help others.

Draw a picture to show how you can say **yes** to God.

We Honor Mary

Jesus told us that
Mary is our mother.
So people all over the
world honor Mary.
Mary is the greatest
of all saints.

Fold

We honor Mary at home.

4

We can honor Mary
in many ways.
When we honor Mary,
we honor Jesus, too.

Fold

We honor Mary in
our churches.

Let's Celebrate

Mary

✝ **We Pray**

Hail Mary, full of grace,
the Lord is with you!

(Raise arms over head.)

Blessed are you among women,
and blessed is the fruit of
    your womb, Jesus.

(Cross arms over heart.)

Holy Mary, Mother of God,
pray for us sinners,

(Put arms down at sides with
palms facing front.)

now and at the hour
    of our death.
Amen.

(Join palms of hands together
to form prayer position.)

PROJECT DISCIPLE

Pray
Learn
Celebrate
Share
Choose
Live

Who is the Mother of God's Son?
Trace the letters.
Color the picture.

Mary

Tell a friend what Mary said to God.

Take Home

Discuss ways you can honor Mary at home and at church.
Decide on one way your family will honor Mary this week.

God the Father Gives Us Jesus

16

WE GATHER

John 3:16

"God so loved the world that he gave [us] his only Son."

What do you give to the people you love?

Jesus is the Son of God.

God is our loving Father.
He loves us very much.
God gives us many gifts.
His greatest gift to us is his Son.
Jesus is God's only Son.

Color every space that has a ♡.
Whose name do you see?

Jesus is one of us.

Jesus was born a long time ago.
He was a baby just as we were.
He grew up.
He had many feelings,
just as we do.

What do you think Jesus
did when he was your age?
Draw what you think he did.

What stories about Jesus do you know?

What is your favorite story?

Look at the pictures. They show ways people learn about Jesus. Color the bows by the pictures of ways you learn about Jesus.

A Package from Grandpa

Look what came today! It's a package from Grandpa. He wrote some clues to help us guess what it is.

Let's open the package. What do you think it is? Oh! It's a Bible!

THE CATHOLIC BIBLE

THE CAT

Fold

Let's Celebrate

God's Gift of Jesus

✝ **We Pray**

🎵 **Jesus in the Morning**

Jesus, Jesus,
Jesus in the morning,
Jesus at the noontime;
Jesus, Jesus,
Jesus when the sun goes down!

Thank him, Thank him,
Thank him in the morning,
Thank him at the noontime;
Thank him, Thank him,
Thank him when the sun
goes down!

God's greatest gift to us is his Son.
Draw him here.

Jesus

www.webelieveweb.com

Take Home

Discuss what you can learn about Jesus from Bible stories
that you know. Finish with a prayer thanking God for the gift
of Jesus, his only Son.

Jesus Grew Up in Nazareth

17

WE GATHER

📖 Luke 2:40

"The child grew and became strong."

How do you grow and become strong? Who helps you to do this?

151

Jesus grew up in a family.

Mary was Jesus' mother.
Joseph was his foster father.

Jesus, Mary, and Joseph
are called the Holy Family.

👤 Draw a ✔ next to the
pictures of the things you
can do with your family.

152

WE BELIEVE

Jesus, Mary, and Joseph showed their love for one another.

The Holy Family lived in Nazareth. Mary and Joseph helped Jesus learn many things. Jesus helped them in their work.

Find what Jesus helped Joseph to make. Connect the dots and color.

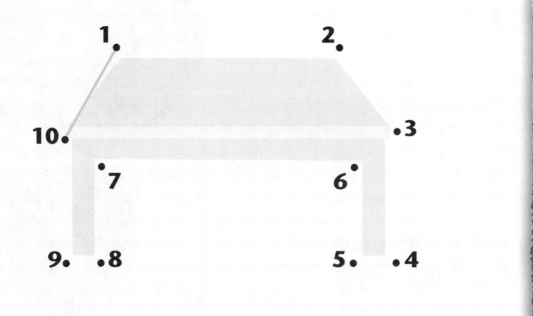

Find what Jesus helped Mary to make. Connect the dots and color.

WE RESPOND

The Holy Family showed their love for God and one another. How can your family do what the Holy Family did?

 Match.

The Holy Family

Your Family

prayed to God everyday

shared stories about God and his people

helped one another learn about God's world

Jesus in the Temple

Luke 2:41–51

Jesus' family went to Jerusalem. They went there to worship God in the Temple. A special feast was being celebrated.

Fold

Finally they found Jesus in the Temple. He was talking to the people about God. Everyone was amazed at how much Jesus knew.

When the celebration was over, Mary and Joseph left. Mary thought Jesus was with Joseph. Joseph thought Jesus was with Mary.

Fold

Later Mary and Joseph could not find Jesus. They were very upset. They returned to Jerusalem. They searched the city for their son.

Let's Celebrate
The Holy Family

✝ **We Pray**

Holy Family, we ask you this day,

- to help us at work
- to help us at play
- to help us at school
- to help us at home
- to help us care for others
- to help us ____.

Holy Family, help us be like you in every way.

PROJECT DISCIPLE

Tell what the Holy Family is doing in each picture.

Draw a way your family does one of these activities.

Take Home

Use the drawing from the completed Project Disciple activity above to discuss ways your own family is like the Holy Family.

Jesus Teaches and Helps Us

WE GATHER

 Matthew 4:23

Jesus went everywhere teaching and helping people.

Look at the picture. How do people help and teach you in each of these places?

159

WE BELIEVE
Jesus taught many people.

When Jesus was a grown-up,
he left his home in Nazareth.

 Matthew 4:23–25

Read Along

Jesus went to many places. Many people listened
to Jesus as he taught about God. People who were
sick, poor, or hungry went to Jesus for help.

Wherever Jesus went, people
came to see him.

Where did Jesus go?
Follow the path to see.
Talk about each place along the way.

WE BELIEVE

Jesus was kind, good, and caring.

Jesus helped people who were sick.
Jesus talked to people.
He listened to them.

📖 Luke 18:15–16

Read Along

Jesus had been teaching all day. People were bringing their children so he could bless them. When Jesus' friends saw this, they tried to stop the people. But Jesus said, "Let the children come to me."

👤 Draw yourself with Jesus.

🎵 Jesus Wants to Help Us

We believe Jesus wants to help us.
We believe Jesus wants to help us.
We believe that Jesus always
  wants to help us.

Ev'ry day Jesus is beside us.
Ev'ry day Jesus is beside us.
We believe that Jesus always
  is beside us.

JESUS JESUS

Loaves and Fish

John 6:3–15

One day thousands of people were listening to Jesus teach. Jesus saw that it was getting late. He knew that the people were hungry.

Fold

Everyone in the crowd had plenty to eat. People were amazed at what Jesus did. They praised and thanked him.

Jesus asked his friends
to find some food.
They found a boy who
had five loaves of bread
and two fish.

Fold

Jesus blessed the
bread and fish.
He gave thanks to God.
Jesus told his friends
to hand out the food.

Let's Celebrate
Jesus

✝ **We Pray**

📖 Luke 18:16

Jesus, you said, "Let the children come to me."

Today we come to you in prayer. Jesus, we thank you for your love. We pray for all the children of the world. We know that you will always help us. Amen.

PROJECT DISCIPLE

Jesus helped people.
Jesus helps us.

Decorate this thank-you card for Jesus.

Thank you Jesus!

Take Home

Remember some of the things that Jesus did for others.
Which of these things can your family do this week?

Jesus Wants Us to Love

WE GATHER

📖 John 15:12

Jesus said, "Love one another as I love you."

Imagine you are in the crowd. What do you hear Jesus saying?

Jesus wants us to tell others we love them.

We can tell other people we love them by the words we say. Sometimes we say, "I love you." Sometimes we can use other words.

How do you feel?

I am sorry.

Can I help you?

� Color around the words that we say to those we love.

Jesus wants us to show others we love them.

Jesus wants us to be kind.
Jesus wants us to share.
Jesus wants us to be fair.
Jesus wants us to listen to one another.

Look at the picture.
Circle the people who are
doing what Jesus wants
us to do.

WE RESPOND

We can ask Jesus
to help us love others.
Ask Jesus to help
you today.

Draw yourself showing love to others.

Saint John Bosco

Saint John Bosco grew up in a poor family in Italy. He helped his family by doing different jobs.

Fold

John started schools where young people learned to do different jobs.
He built places for them to work.
John's kindness showed the young people how to love God and others.

John wanted to tell people
about God.
So he learned how to juggle.
When people came to
watch him, John told them
about God's love.

Fold

When John was older,
he became a priest.
He helped many poor
and homeless children.
He found places for them
to live, work, and pray.

Let's Celebrate
God's Gift of Love

✝ **We Pray**

🎵 **Listen to Jesus**

Alleluia, alleluia,
    alleluia, alleluia!
Listen to Jesus.
Do what he tells you.

Open your hearts today.

Live in God's love today.

Color the spaces with ♥  red .
Color the picture.

What does Jesus want us to do?

Take Home

Talk about ways your family members show love to each other. Then discuss how it makes each of you feel to show love and to receive love.

Lent

Advent Christmas Ordinary Time **Lent** Three Days Easter Ordinary Time

WE GATHER

Matthew 17:5

"This is my beloved Son, with whom I am well pleased; listen to him."

When do you listen to Jesus?

Jesus asks us to live as he did.

Jesus showed us how to live.
He wants us to love God and others.
There is a special time of year when we
try to do this.

We celebrate Lent.

During this special time we pray.
We try to act as Jesus did.
We find ways to care for others.

Jesus cared for everyone.
Many people care for you.
You can care for them, too.

Act out a way you can show them you care.

A Special Time for Jesus

We learn about Jesus.

Fold

We help others as Jesus did.

4

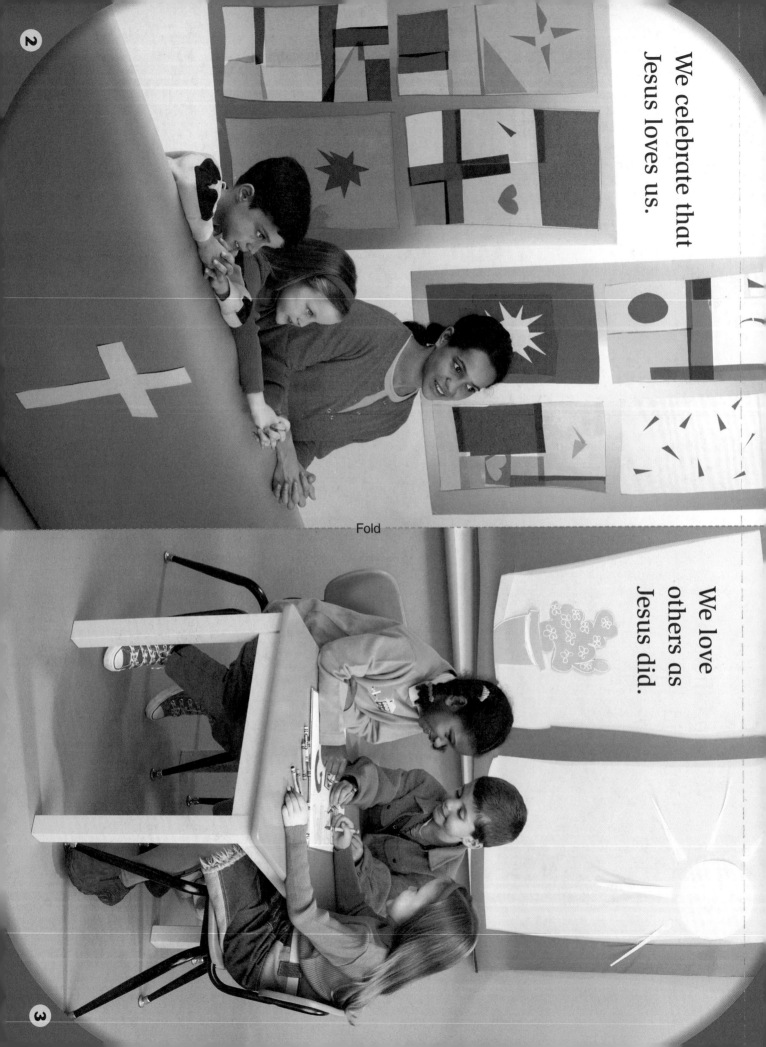

We celebrate that Jesus loves us.

Fold

We love others as Jesus did.

Let's Celebrate
Our Friend Jesus

✝ **We Pray**

🎵 **I Am Your Friend**

Chorus

I am your friend,
always here beside you,
to watch and be with you
in all that you do.
I am your friend,
I am your friend.

Jesus helps us ev'ry day
in the fears that come our way,
in our hearts we hear him say: (Chorus)

Color the shapes next to the pictures that show people celebrating Lent.

Take Home

During Lent families can make a special effort to care for each other. Discuss ways the members of your family can care for each other.

The Three Days

21

WE GATHER

John 3:16

"God so loved the world."

What days are very important to you?

183

The Three Days are very special.

Jesus loved us so much!
He gave his whole life for us.
We celebrate this in a special way
on the Three Days.

We celebrate the Three Days.

Thank Jesus for his love.

 Write your name on the banner.

 Draw a picture to show that you love Jesus.

The Greatest Days

We celebrate three
great days.
We pray and show
God our love.

We celebrate that
Jesus loves us.
Alleluia!

Fold

Let's Celebrate
The Three Days

✝ **We Pray**

🎵 **Sing for Joy**

Sing and jump for joy, alleluia!
Sing and jump for joy, alleluia!
Sing and jump for joy, alleluia!
Alleluia! Alleluia!

Sing and dance for joy, alleluia!
Sing and dance for joy, alleluia!
Sing and dance for joy, alleluia!
Alleluia! Alleluia!

PROJECT DISCIPLE

The cross is decorated with flowers.
Color the flowers to show that the
Three Days are very special.

Take Home

Discuss ways that your family can demonstrate love for
Jesus. As a family pray, *Jesus, thank you for loving us. We
love you.*

Jesus Wants Us to Share God's Love

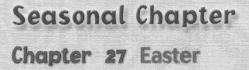

Seasonal Chapter

DEAR FAMILY

In Unit 4 your child will grow as a disciple of Jesus by:

- recognizing that through Baptism we belong to God's family, the Church
- praying as Jesus did
- celebrating with the Church at Mass
- learning ways we can show our love for God and others
- appreciating Jesus as our friend.

Make it Happen

At the end of Mass, the priest dismisses us. Talk about what your family will do after Mass on Sunday to love and serve the Lord and others.

Celebrate!

Tell your child about his or her Baptism. Share any mementos you have: photos, videos, Baptismal candle, white garment. Consider sharing your own Baptism story, too. Where were you baptized? by whom? Contact your own and your child's godparents—by letter, card, e-mail, or phone.

Reality Check

"The family should live in such a way that its members learn to care and take responsibility for the young, the old, the sick, the handicapped, and the poor."

(*Catechism of the Catholic Church*, 2208)

Fast Facts

According to the 2009 Pontifical Year-book, there were 1.147 billion Catholics worldwide at the end of 2007. A 2007 census showed there were 67 million Catholics in the United States. Help your child to appreciate how many people throughout the world share our faith!

Pray Today

Begin teaching your child the simple responses we say at Mass to help him or her participate. Use the *We Pray at Mass* booklet your child makes in Chapter 24.

Take Home

Each chapter in your child's *We Believe* Kindergarten text offers a "Take Home" activity that invites your family to support your child's journey to more fully become a disciple of Christ.

Be ready for this unit's Take Home:

Chapter 22: Praying the Sign of the Cross

Chapter 23: Integrating prayer into family life

Chapter 24: Celebrating at Mass

Chapter 25: Caring for others

Chapter 26: Remembering that Jesus is always with your family

We Belong to the Church

WE GATHER

📖 1 John 3:1

See what love the Father has given us. "We may be called the children of God."

Look at the people in each place.
Why are they together?

193

The Church is the family of God.

God loves us very much.
He wants each of us to be part
of his family.
God's special family is the Church.
The Church is all over the world.

Draw your family as part of
God's family.

At Baptism we become members of the Church.

Baptism is the beginning of our new life in God's family.
Look at the picture.
At Baptism the priest or deacon says these words while he pours the water.

"____, I baptize you in the name of the Father,
and of the Son,
and of the Holy Spirit."

Water is a sign of life.
Color this sign of life.

WE RESPOND

You were baptized.
You were welcomed into the Church.
The priest or deacon poured
water over you.
He said,

"_____

_____

_____
(name)

I baptize you in the name of the Father,
and of the Son,
and of the Holy Spirit."

⟨X⟩ Put a picture of your Baptism here.

The Sign of the Cross

We can learn a special prayer. It is called the Sign of the Cross. We can pray it anywhere.

Fold

Pray the Sign of the Cross. Pray it often.

4

1. In the name of the Father,

2. and of the Son,

Here is the way we pray the Sign of the Cross.

Fold

3. and of the Holy

4. Spirit.

5. Amen.

Let's Celebrate

Belonging to the Church

✝ **We Pray**

♫ God Is a Part of My Life

God is a part of my life.
God is a part of my life.
God is a part of my life.
I rejoice, I rejoice, I rejoice.

I am a part of God's life!
I am a part of God's life!
I am a part, I belong to
 God's family.
I am a part of God's life!

Pray
Learn
Celebrate
Share
Choose
Live

Trace the numbers next to each part of the prayer.
Pray the Sign of the Cross.

1

2

3

4

5

www.webelieveweb.com

Take Home

Pray as a family, *God, thank you for inviting us into your family.* Begin and end with the Sign of the Cross.

We Pray As Jesus Did

WE GATHER

📖 Jeremiah 29:12

When you pray to me, I will listen.

Look at the pictures.

What is the same?
What is different?

Prayer is one way we can show our love for God.

Prayer is listening to and talking to God.
We can pray to God anytime.
We can pray to him anywhere.
We can talk to God about anything we want.

Draw a picture of yourself praying.

WE BELIEVE

Jesus showed us how to pray.

In the Bible we can read about Jesus praying. He prayed everywhere:

- with his family and friends
- outdoors
- at celebrations
- in holy places.

Jesus wants us to pray, too.

We can pray by ourselves. We can pray with other people. Put a ✔ next to the pictures that show where you pray with others.

Here is a prayer that Jesus taught us.

The Lord's Prayer

Our Father, who art in heaven,
hallowed be thy name;
thy kingdom come;
thy will be done on earth
   as it is in heaven.
Give us this day our daily bread;
and forgive us our trespasses
as we forgive those
   who trespass against us;
and lead us not into temptation,
but deliver us from evil. Amen.

Color in the name of this prayer.

Now that I can pray myself, there are many things I want to say.

Fold

God, bless my family and my friends. Bless the people who are hungry or sick. Please keep us all close to you.

Let's Celebrate
Praying to God

✝ **We Pray**

Alleluia is a joyful prayer to God.

🎵 **Sing for Joy**

Sing and shout for joy, alleluia!
Sing and shout for joy, alleluia!
Sing and shout for joy, alleluia!
Alleluia! Alleluia!

Sing and clap your hands, alleluia!
Sing and clap your hands, alleluia!
Sing and clap your hands, alleluia!
Alleluia! Alleluia!

Sing and jump for joy, alleluia!
Sing and jump for joy, alleluia!
Sing and jump for joy, alleluia!
Alleluia! Alleluia!

Listen to the story.
Color the picture.

Read Along

Blessed Kateri Tekakwitha was a Native American.
She taught children prayers.
She shared stories about Jesus.
Kateri prayed, "Jesus, I love you."

Take Home

Integrate prayer into your family's daily life. Pray at meals,
pray to begin and end the day, and pray always in moments
of joy and sorrow.

We Celebrate Jesus' Gift of Himself

WE GATHER

📖 Luke 22:17

Jesus said,
"Take this and share it."

Act out what people say and do at celebrations.

Jesus shared a special meal with his friends.

Jack Savitsky, artist *Last Supper*

We call this special meal the Last Supper.
At this meal Jesus prayed with his friends.
Together they thanked God.
Jesus blessed bread and wine.
This bread and wine became the Body
and Blood of Jesus.

Jesus gave the gift of himself to his
friends at the

LAST SUPPER

Jesus shares himself with us, too.

The Mass is a special celebration.
We thank God for his gifts.
We remember Jesus in a special way.
At Mass the priest blesses bread and wine.
The bread and wine become the Body and Blood of Jesus.

 Jesus gives us the gift of himself at

MASS

WE RESPOND

Think about the many gifts
God has given to you.
Thank him by singing.

♫ Celebrate God

Chorus
Celebrate God with your hands.
Celebrate God with your voice.
Celebrate God in all that you do.
And God will be with you.

Listen to God with your mind.
Listen to God in your heart.
Listen to God speaking with you.
And God will be with you. (Chorus)

We Pray at Mass

At Mass we thank and praise God.
We sing songs together.
We sing, "Glory to God."

The priest blesses us.
He tells us to love God and others.
We say, "Thanks be to God."

The priest or deacon reads to us about Jesus. We listen carefully. We say, "**Praise to you, Lord Jesus Christ.**"

Fold

The priest prays over the bread and wine. The bread and wine become the Body and Blood of Jesus. Together we remember what Jesus has done. The priest prays and thanks God. We sing, "**Amen.**"

Let's Celebrate

Jesus' Gift of Himself

✝ We Pray

Thank you, Jesus, for sharing yourself with us.
Jesus, we thank you.

Thank you, Jesus, for the gift of yourself at Mass.
Jesus, we thank you.

Thank you, Jesus, for being with us always.
Jesus, we thank you.

PROJECT DISCIPLE

Pray
Learn
Celebrate
Share
Choose
Live

What are the people in the picture doing?

Add yourself to the picture.

Take Home

Discuss the things we do at Mass including thanking God for his gifts, remembering Jesus, singing songs, and listening to stories about Jesus. Attend a family Mass and notice all the ways people celebrate.

We Care About Others As Jesus Did

25

WE GATHER

📖 John 13:15

Jesus said to his friends, "As I have done for you, you should also do."

How can you help others?

217

Jesus cared about everyone.

Jesus fed people who were hungry.
Jesus helped people who were poor or sick.
Jesus made those who were sad or
lonely feel better.
Jesus showed us how to care for everyone.

Color the path Jesus walked.
Circle the people whom Jesus helped.

Jesus wants us to care about others, too.

Jesus wants us to help people who are in need.

Jesus wants us to help people who are poor, sick, or lonely.

How can you show you care for someone?

✖ Match to show what you can do.

There are many ways to show
we care about others.
Think about someone you know.
How can you show you care?

♪ Caring for Others
("Mary Had a Little Lamb")

Jesus cares for everyone,
everyone, everyone.
We can care for everyone
just as Jesus did.

When we help, we show we care,
show we care, show we care.
When we give, we show
   we care
just as Jesus did.

The Caring Man

📖 Luke 10:29–37

Jesus told this story.
One day a man was walking
down a road.
Robbers came along.
They beat him and
took his money.
They left him hurt
and alone.

Fold

Who was the caring
man in this story?
How did he show
that he cared?

Some people walked by the man who was hurt. But they did not stop to help him.

Later, another man came walking down the road. He stopped and helped the man who was hurt.

Let's Celebrate

Caring as Jesus Did

✝ **We Pray**

Jesus, you helped others.
Jesus, help us to be like you.

Jesus, you cared for others.
Jesus, help us to be like you.

Jesus, you _____.
Jesus, help us to be like you.

PROJECT DISCIPLE

 Pray Learn Celebrate Share Choose Live

Draw a ✔ next to the pictures that show children caring for others.

Which is your favorite picture?

Take Home

Brainstorm ways your family can help care for others. Try to do five good deeds. Once you have met your goal, have a family celebration.

We Celebrate That Jesus Is Our Friend

26

WE GATHER

📖 John 15:15

Jesus told us that he calls us friends.

How do you spend time with your friends?

WE BELIEVE

Jesus had many friends.

Jesus liked to spend time with his friends.
Here is a story about one of those times.

📖 John 21:4–13

Read Along

One morning Jesus' friends were on a boat fishing.
They looked up. They saw a man standing on the shore.
Someone shouted that it was Jesus. The friends hurried
to get to the shore. Jesus had fish and bread ready for them.
Jesus said to his friends, "Come, have breakfast." (John 21:12)
The friends sat down and ate with Jesus.

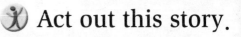 Act out this story.

226

Jesus shares his friendship with us.

📖 Matthew 28:20

Jesus said, "I am with you always."

Jesus is with us when we are by ourselves.
He is with us when we are with our families.
He is with us when we are with our friends.
Jesus is always with us.

I am with you always.

🚶 What does your friend Jesus say to you?
Color the words of the message.

WE RESPOND

How can you thank Jesus for being your friend?

Pray.

Be kind.

Help others.

Share.

Be fair.

 Color the shells to show what you will do.

Always with us

Bubbles float away.

But Jesus is with us always.

Fold

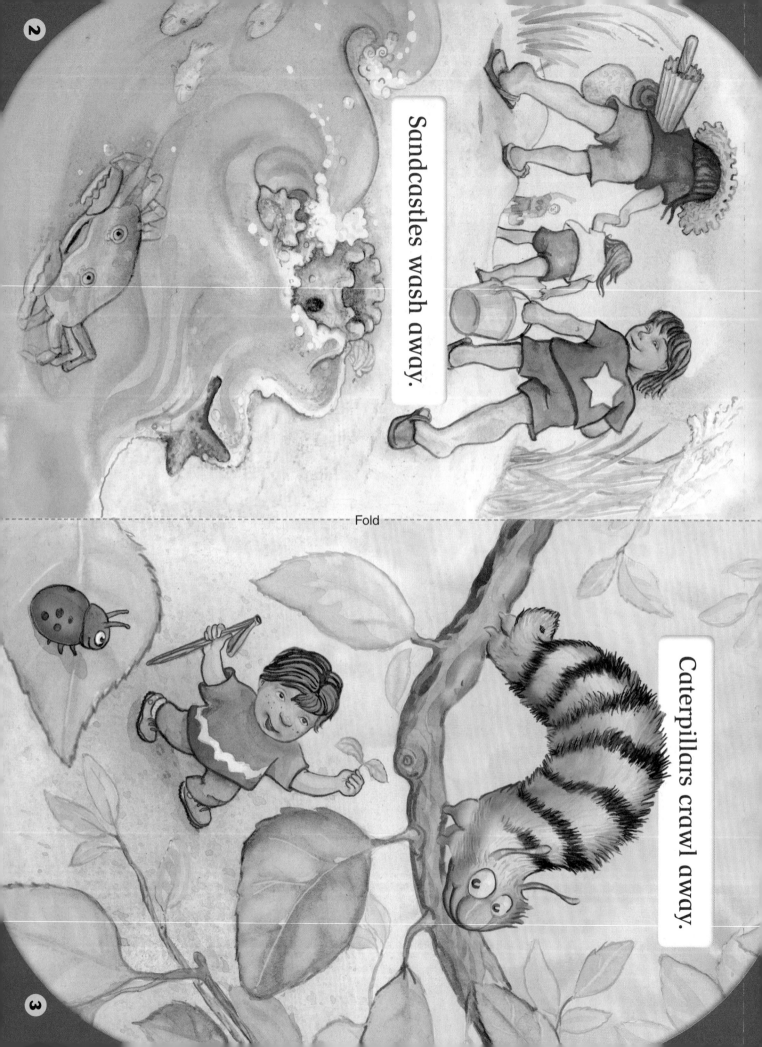

Sandcastles wash away.

Caterpillars crawl away.

Let's Celebrate

Jesus Is Our Friend

✝ **We Pray**

♫ Jesus in the Morning

Jesus, Jesus,
Jesus in the morning,
Jesus at the noontime.
Jesus, Jesus,
Jesus when the sun goes down!

Love him, love him,
love him in the morning,
Love him at the noontime.
Love him, love him,
love him when the sun goes down!

PROJECT DISCIPLE

Color the spaces with 1 red.
Color the spaces with 2 blue.
Color the spaces with 3 yellow.
Color the spaces with 4 green.

When is Jesus with us? Tell a friend.

Take Home

Discuss times when you might feel lonely, sad, or in need of a friend. Discuss ways that Jesus can help during those times. Remember that Jesus is always with your family!

Easter

27

Advent | Christmas | Ordinary Time | Lent | Three Days | Easter | Ordinary Time

WE GATHER

 Psalm 149:1

"Sing to the LORD
a new song."

What does this picture
make you think of?

We celebrate Jesus' new life.

Jesus is so wonderful.
We celebrate his love and his life.

What signs of life do you see around you? Draw some here.

We celebrate Easter.

We celebrate Jesus' new life.
We give thanks for the new life Jesus brings us.

Color the word to complete the sentence.

We celebrate new life together during

Easter.

WE RESPOND

Think about ways families celebrate Easter.

 Draw your family and friends celebrating Easter.

We Celebrate New Life

Alleluia!

Fold

Alleluia! Alleluia! Alleluia!

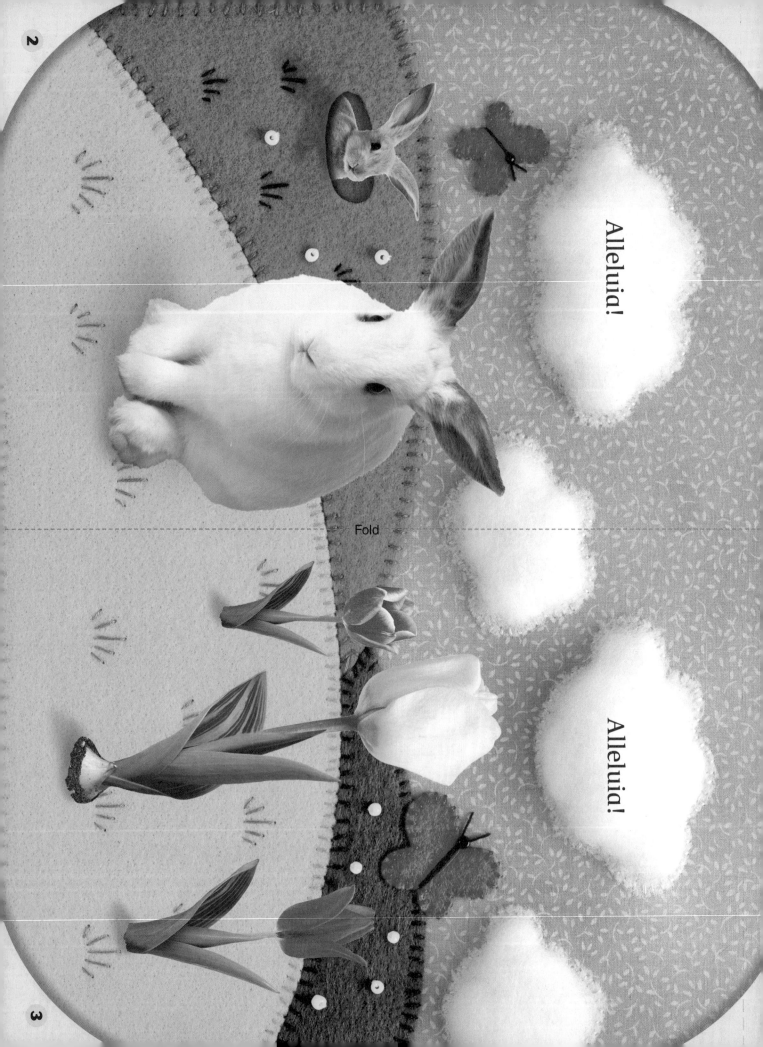

Alleluia!

Alleluia!

Fold

2

3

Let's Celebrate

Easter

✝ **We Pray**

♪ **Sing a New Song**

Sing a new song unto the Lord;
let your song be sung
from mountains high.
Sing a new song unto the Lord,
singing alleluia.

PROJECT DISCIPLE

Pray
Learn
Celebrate
Share
Choose
Live

Trace the message
Decorate the Easter poster
with signs of life.

Happy Easter

Share your poster with others.

Take Home

With your family, plant and nurture a seed with soil, water, and sunlight. Watch it grow and let it remind your family to celebrate the new life of Jesus.

Pray
Learn
Celebrate
Share
Choose
Live

God's Great Gifts

Read Along

Grammy took Jason by the hand. "I have a surprise for you," she said. "Do you remember the seeds we planted?" Jason nodded his head. It seemed like that was a long, long time ago.

Jason and his grandmother walked to the garden. They went to the place where he and Grammy had dug a hole and put in the seeds. There Jason saw a bright red flower.

Jason laughed and jumped in the air. "We did it, Grammy! We grew flowers!" Grammy smiled. "We planted the seeds," she said. "God made the flowers grow. Let's tell God how happy we are."

Jason and his grandmother sat down on a bench. Grammy prayed, "We are so happy, God. You fill our world with good things." Jason thought, "God made Grammy, too." That made Jason even happier!

What makes you happy?

Because *We Believe*

God made all things.
They make us happy.

We thank God for all his gifts.

All things are gifts from God. What good things do you see around you?

Name or draw one of your favorite things.

Talk about ways that your family can thank God for all his gifts.

Look for something in your home that makes you want to thank God.

Tell a story about why it is so special.

Pray Together

Dear God,
Thank you for

_____

_____

Amen.

PROJECT DISCIPLE

Pray Learn Celebrate Share Choose Live

Family Fun

Look at the pictures.

What things can families do to have fun?

Because *We Believe*

Families have special ways to share God's love.

God wants families to spend time together.

243

God helps us to be safe.

Name people in your neighborhood who help keep us safe.

What are ways our families help keep us safe?

Talk about ways families can share God's love.

Share one place your family has fun together.

Share one place your family prays together.

Pray Together

Strong and faithful God, keep our family safe from harm. Make us a blessing to all those we meet today.

Amen.

Adapted from *Catholic Household Blessings and Prayers*

PROJECT DISCIPLE

Doing What Jesus Wants Us to Do

Read Along

Katie's mother is tired. She has worked hard all day. Now it is time to fix dinner.

Katie wants to go outside to play. Her friend, Carla, has a new bike. Carla said she would let Katie ride it.

Katie thinks to herself. She then goes into the kitchen.

"Mama, can I help set the table?" Katie asks.

Pray
Learn
Celebrate
Share
Choose
Live

How did Katie help her mother?

Because *We Believe*

Jesus helped many people.

Jesus wants us to be kind and caring.

245

Jesus wants us to love and help one another.

Think of one way you can help someone when you are:

- at school
- on the playground
- in church
- at a store.

 Write two other places you can help someone.

_____

_____

Talk about the ways Jesus wants us to love each other.

Pray Together

Make up a prayer with your family.

Ask Jesus to help you be kind and loving to one another.

The Holy Spirit Came

Jesus promised to send the Holy Spirit. Mary and the friends of Jesus waited. They prayed together.

They went out to tell all the people about Jesus.

2

The Holy Spirit came.

Mary and the friends of Jesus were very happy.

3

My Prayer Book

Fold

Sign of the Cross

In the name of the Father,
and of the Son,
and of the Holy Spirit.
Amen.

Fold

Grace After Meals

We give you thanks, almighty God,
for these and all your gifts
which we have received
through Christ our Lord.
Amen.

Our Father

Our Father, who art in heaven,
hallowed be thy name;
thy kingdom come;
thy will be done on earth
as it is in heaven.
Give us this day our daily bread;
and forgive us our trespasses
as we forgive those who trespass
against us;
and lead us not into temptation,
but deliver us from evil.

Amen.

- - - Fold - - -

Grace Before Meals

Bless us, O Lord,
and these your gifts,
which we are about to receive
from your goodness.
Through Christ our Lord.

Amen.

Hail Mary

Hail Mary, full of grace,
the Lord is with you!
Blessed are you among women,
and blessed is the fruit of
     your womb, Jesus.
Holy Mary, Mother of God,
pray for us sinners,
now and at the hour of our death.
Amen.

Fold

Glory Be to the Father

Glory be to the Father
and to the Son
and to the Holy Spirit,
as it was in the beginning
is now, and ever shall be
world without end.
Amen.

Index

The following is a list of topics that appear in the pupil's text.
Boldface indicates an entire chapter.

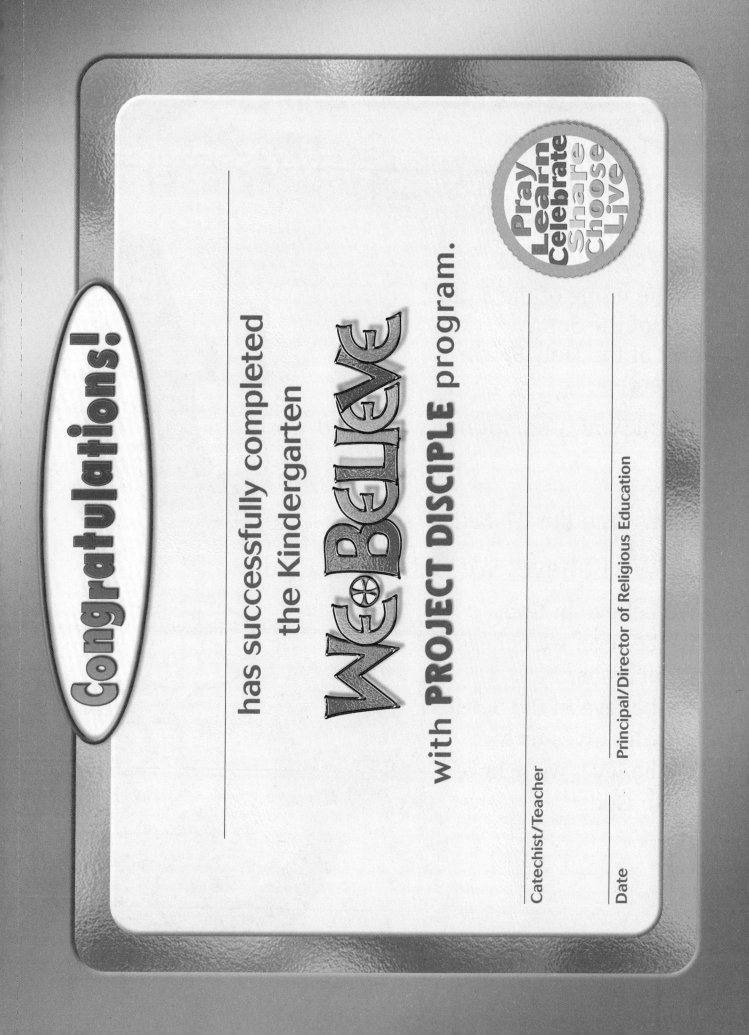

Congratulations!

has successfully completed

the Kindergarten

We Believe

with **PROJECT DISCIPLE** program.

Pray
Learn
Celebrate
Share
Choose
Live

Catechist/Teacher

Date

Principal/Director of Religious Education

End-of-Year Prayer Service

✝ We Pray

In the name of the Father,
and of the Son,
and of the Holy Spirit.
Amen.

Thank you, God, for our wonderful world.

Let us sing the *We Believe* song.

🎵 We Believe, We Believe in God

We believe in God;
We believe, we believe
   in Jesus;
We believe in the Spirit
   who gives us life.
We believe, we believe
   in God.

See you next year!